MAXIMUM
FLAVOR

MAXIMUM FLAVOR

Recipes That Will Change the Way You Cook

AKI KAMOZAWA & H. ALEXANDER TALBOT

Clarkson Potter/Publishers
New York

Published in the United States by Clarkson Potter/
Publishers, an imprint of the Crown Publishing
Group, a division of Random House, Inc., New York.
www.crownpublishing.com
www.clarksonpotter.com

CLARKSON POTTER is a trademark and POTTER
with colophon is a registered trademark of Random
House, Inc.

Library of Congress Cataloging-in-Publication Data
Kamozawa, Aki.
  Maximum flavor/Aki Kamozawa and H. Alexander
Talbot.
     pages cm
  Includes index.
  1. Cooking. 2. Cookbooks. lcgft I. Talbot, H.
Alexander. II. Title.
  TX714.K3578 2013
  641.5—dc23
                                    2012033801
ISBN 978-0-7704-3321-5
eISBN 978-0-7704-3322-2

Printed in China

BOOK DESIGN: Laura Palese

10   9   8   7   6   5   4   3   2   1

First Edition

For those who
**KNOW US WELL
& LOVE US ANYWAY**

because you
**INSPIRE US TO
DO MORE**

CONTENTS

INTRODUCTION

WE LOVE TO PLAY WITH FOOD. In fact, we love it so much that we've made careers out of it. When we cooked professionally, we started experimenting in our free time, teaching ourselves new approaches and embracing innovation to make food taste better. We eventually made the jump to opening our own business and now consult with restaurants and companies big and small to help them solve kitchen conundrums and think more creatively about cooking.

As a result, you'll find lots of kitchen science in these pages. When, years ago, we became fascinated by figuring out the hows and whys of what happens in the kitchen, we started chronicling our adventures on our website and blog, *Ideas in Food*. Modern cooking, aka molecular gastronomy, has inspired many chefs and cooks to explore new ideas in the kitchen, which is always a good thing. But some of its techniques can be too over the top for most home cooks—like using liquid nitrogen to freeze ice cream. So in this book we focus exclusively on recipes that can help home cooks make better meals every day. And while there are many cool things you can do with food, we're only ever interested in the tricks and techniques that help deliver maximum flavor.

Often we'll take a standard recipe and see if we can improve it by experimenting with different ways to prepare it. When you make French Fries (page 123), for example, conventional wisdom is to soak the cut potatoes and then deep-fry them twice in oil, once at a lower temperature and then a second time at a higher one. We found that several tweaks resulted in fries that are always golden and crisp on the outside and tender on the inside: soaking in salted water, steaming the potatoes to hydrate the starches, and then frying just once to brown the exterior. And if you want a great burger alongside, check out our Butter Burgers (page 166), which also break some culinary rules; contrary to popular belief, burgers cook more quickly and evenly if you flip them regularly.

We also use pantry ingredients strategically to maximize flavor. It turns out that the secret to the best Korean-Style Chicken Wings (page 156) starts with a simple marinade of egg whites, baking soda, and salt,

while there are many
COOL THINGS YOU CAN DO WITH FOOD,
↳ we're only ever interested in the
TRICKS & TECHNIQUES THAT HELP DELIVER MAXIMUM FLAVOR

which not only seasons them but also starts to break down the proteins on the skin, resulting in juicy wings with a thin, crackling exterior. Tapioca takes the place of eggs in Banana Caramel Ice Cream (page 243), making it smooth and creamy while keeping the flavor strong and pure. And we discovered a great way to get even more oomph out of nuts: Cook them in a simple sugar syrup first, allowing them to soak in the liquid, before toasting them as you normally would. The nuts take on a deep, dark brown color and have a rich flavor and an excellent crunch (page 39).

In many recipes, we take advantage of common kitchen equipment that home cooks may otherwise overlook. Take the microwave. This often-maligned machine is actually very useful. We put it to use in making cheese "Danishes" (page 30), which sounds odd, but you end up with a lightness in texture that isn't possible to achieve in a regular oven. Another piece of equipment that we champion is the pressure cooker, which is not as scary as it may sound. It speeds up some cooking processes so much that it's much easier to make, for example, delicious baked beans (page 72) on a weeknight, since the pressure cooker decreases the unattended cooking time to just under an hour. And in recent years, there's been lots of talk about sous vide, which is basically using a water bath to cook food precisely to a specific temperature—no more, no less. Using this technique at home—whether with a formal setup or just by using zip-top bags and a pot of water—you never need to worry about overcooking expensive cuts of meat; in fact, our favorite way of cooking a porterhouse is to cook it first sous vide and then grill the meat, producing a perfectly tender juicy steak with that all-important char on the outside (page 177).

We want *Maximum Flavor* to be a helpful kitchen guide and a source of inspiration. So not only does each recipe offer some sort of insight into how food works and how you can make it taste better, but, throughout the book, we've also included sidebars with discussions on topics such as gluten-free mixes for baking, how to balance salty and sweet flavors, and what fermentation is and how it makes sourdough so delicious—all to help inform your day-to-day cooking.

You'll find that measurements in the ingredients lists are given in standard American volume measurements and also by weight in grams. The volume, or imperial, measurements are the ones with which most home cooks are more comfortable, and we want everyone to cook from this book. That said, using the gram measurements will provide the most accuracy, and we strongly encourage the use of a scale for all of the recipes with an emphasis on baking; volume measurements for ingredients such as flour, cornstarch, and confectioners' sugar vary greatly as the ingredients tend to get packed down in their containers.

We hope that *Maximum Flavor* gives you lots of interesting ideas and helpful information to boost your own kitchen creativity. The recipes in this book can be adapted and altered to suit your own palate, and the techniques can be applied to other dishes (the handy freezer shucking tip in the New England Clam Chowder recipe on page 69 just may make cooking quick seafood dishes on a weeknight more of a reality in your house, too).

SO EXPERIMENT, TASTE, PLAY WITH YOUR FOOD,

and discover again why cooking and eating are so fascinating and fun.

1

BREAKFAST

CLASSIC DEVILED EGGS ARE ALWAYS A FAVORITE, BUT THEY can be a challenge to pull off perfectly every time. We prefer the technique of steaming eggs to hard cooking them, because it gives consistent results with the added benefit of making the eggs easier to peel—meaning you can say good-bye forever to that green tinge around the yolk and also to whites that are pitted and unattractive to set out. The smoked tea brine bath seasons the eggs after they're cooked and makes them look beautiful and festive. Leftover pickle juice (or olive brine) is often thoughtlessly discarded but makes an inspiring addition to dishes such as this one. The glazed bacon is crisp, sweet, spicy, and the perfect accent to the creamy eggs.

MAKES 24 DEVILED EGGS

BACON & DEVILED EGGS

DEVILED EGGS

12 large **eggs**

4 cups / 907 grams **cranberry juice**

½ ounce / 15 grams **Lapsang Souchong tea** (about 6 tea bags)

1 tablespoon / 18 grams **fine sea salt**

½ cup / 100 grams **mayonnaise,** preferably Duke's or Hellmann's

1 tablespoon / 14 grams **Dijon mustard**

1 tablespoon / 14 grams **sweet pickle juice**

2 tablespoons / 43 grams **red pepper jelly**

COOK AND BRINE THE EGGS: Set a stovetop steamer over high heat and bring the water to a boil. Put the eggs in the steamer basket, add them to the pot, cover, and steam the eggs for 14 minutes. While the eggs are steaming, prepare an ice water bath. When the eggs are cooked, transfer them to the ice water and let cool for about 15 minutes.

Meanwhile, in a large bowl, combine the cranberry juice, tea, and salt, stirring until the salt is dissolved.

Take the eggs out of the ice water, and use the back of a spoon to uniformly crack the shells all over without piercing the eggs or removing any of the shell. Put the cracked eggs into the brine and put another bowl on top of the eggs to keep them submerged. Refrigerate the eggs for 48 hours.

After 48 hours, take the eggs out of the brine and peel them, discarding the shells. Halve each egg lengthwise. Remove the yolks and set the whites aside. In a small food processor, combine the egg yolks, mayonnaise, mustard, and pickle juice and puree until smooth. Scoop the deviled egg mixture into a pastry bag fitted with a star tip and put the bag in the refrigerator.

(recipe continues)

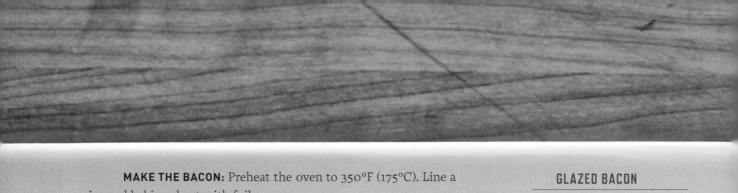

MAKE THE BACON: Preheat the oven to 350°F (175°C). Line a rimmed baking sheet with foil.

Lay the bacon slices on a cutting board. Brush one side of each slice with some of the pepper jelly and then lay the slices glaze side up on a wire rack set over the foil-lined pan. Bake the bacon for 15 minutes, or until just crispy and glazed. Remove the bacon from the oven, brush both sides of the bacon with more of the jelly, and put it back in the oven for 3 more minutes. Remove the bacon from the oven and let cool. Cut each slice of bacon into 4 pieces so that you have 1 piece for each deviled egg.

GLAZED BACON

6 slices **bacon**

¼ cup / 85 grams **red pepper jelly**

ASSEMBLE THE EGGS: Put the egg whites on a cutting board or other flat work surface. Spoon ¼ teaspoon pepper jelly into the bottom of each egg white. Pipe a rosette (about 1 tablespoon) of the egg yolk mixture on top of the jelly. Top with a slice of bacon. Arrange the deviled eggs on a cutting board or platter to serve.

PASTA CARBONARA IS A TRADITIONAL DISH OF NOODLES TOSSED with eggs, cheese, and pancetta, finished with coarsely ground black pepper. It was easy for us to picture this for breakfast, substituting oatmeal for the pasta. We like to combine different types of oatmeal and toast the grains to create porridge with texture and substance. Steaming the eggs re-creates the experience of soft-boiled eggs without the hassle of dealing with the shell at the table. When you cut into the egg with your spoon, the warm yolk runs out and makes a sauce for the dish. We've found that people who claim they don't like oatmeal often succumb to the charms of this breakfast.

SERVES 4 TO 6

8 large cold **eggs**

½ cup / 80 grams **steel-cut oats**

½ cup / 50 grams **rolled oats**

½ cup / 55 grams **oat bran**

3⅔ cups / 820 grams **chicken** or **vegetable stock**

1 medium **onion,** chopped

½ teaspoon / 3 grams **fine sea salt**

8.8 ounces / 250 grams **pancetta,** chopped

½ bunch / 50 grams **scallions,** thinly sliced

6 tablespoons / 36 grams freshly grated **Parmigiano Reggiano cheese**

Fleur de sel and **freshly ground black pepper**

OATMEAL CARBONARA

Set a stovetop steamer over high heat and bring the water to a boil. Put the eggs in the steamer basket, add to the pot, cover, and cook for 7 minutes. While the eggs are steaming, prepare an ice water bath.

When the eggs are cooked, transfer them to the ice water and let the eggs cool for 20 minutes. Take them out, use the back of a spoon to gently crack the shells, and return them to the ice water for 10 more minutes to make them easier to peel. Remove the eggs from the water and peel them carefully—they are delicate with a runny yolk. The eggs can be made ahead and stored in a covered container in the refrigerator for up to 2 days.

Preheat the oven to 350°F (175°C). Line a baking sheet with parchment paper.

Put the steel-cut oats, rolled oats, and oat bran on the baking sheet. Toast the oats in the oven until they are golden brown, about 5 minutes. Transfer the oats to a bowl that fits inside your pressure cooker and then add the stock, onion, and salt. Stir well.

Put 1 inch (2.5 cm) of water and a small rack in the bottom of the pressure cooker. Set the bowl on the rack and pressure-cook for 5 minutes at high pressure. Once the oats have finished cooking, let the pressure dissipate naturally and remove the lid. Carefully remove the bowl from inside the pressure cooker. Stir the oatmeal a few times and let it rest.

Meanwhile, pulse the pancetta in a food processor until it is minced; do not let it become a puree. Using a rubber spatula, scrape the pancetta into a medium cast-iron skillet and set over low heat. Cook, stirring often to prevent sticking, until the fat renders out and the pancetta becomes crispy, 8 to 10 minutes. Strain the pancetta, catching the fat in a heatproof container, then spread the pancetta out on a paper towel–lined plate, and let cool. Reserve the fat separately in a covered container in the refrigerator for up to 2 weeks. The rendered fat can be used for cooking, or you can fold it into the finished carbonara for extra richness and flavor.

Reheat the eggs by putting a large pot of water over medium heat and bringing it up to 140°F (60°C). Remove the pot from the heat and slide in the eggs. Let the eggs warm in the hot water for 10 minutes. Use a slotted spoon to remove the eggs from the water and pat them dry.

Stir the crispy pancetta, scallions, and Parmigiano Reggiano into the oatmeal. Spoon the oatmeal into bowls, making a small indentation in the center of each bowl. Nestle a steamed egg in the indentation. Sprinkle the egg with fleur de sel and grind black pepper over the entire dish. Serve immediately.

THE SPICY SCENT OF GINGER WAFTING THROUGH THE HOUSE makes these waffles the perfect choice to lure people out of bed on a cold winter morning. We add a blend of spices including chili powder to round out the flavor of the ginger and accentuate its natural heat. The white whole wheat and barley flours lend a wonderful nutty flavor while retaining a light texture. If you prefer a heartier texture you can easily substitute whole wheat flour for the white wheat, or you can use all-purpose flour if you prefer a more delicate waffle. The batter can be made up to an hour in advance and kept at room temperature until you are ready to cook. If the batter gets a little too thick, simply add a tablespoon or two of buttermilk to thin it out.

MAKES 10 TO 12 WAFFLES

GINGERBREAD WAFFLES

1½ cups / 210 grams **white whole wheat flour**

½ cup / 70 grams **barley flour**

½ teaspoon / 2.5 grams **baking soda**

½ teaspoon / 3 grams **fine sea salt**

1 teaspoon / 2.5 grams **ground ginger**

¼ teaspoon / 0.5 gram **ground cloves**

¼ teaspoon / 0.5 gram **ground cinnamon**

¼ teaspoon / 0.5 gram **chili powder**

2 large **eggs**

¼ cup / 100 grams **unsulphured blackstrap molasses**

2 cups / 480 grams **cultured buttermilk,** homemade (page 54) or store-bought

Preheat a waffle iron.

In a medium bowl, whisk together the white whole wheat flour, barley flour, baking soda, salt, ginger, cloves, cinnamon, and chili powder. Add the eggs, molasses, and buttermilk and whisk together lightly before slowly incorporating the flour until you have a stiff but still fluid batter. Let the batter rest for at least 5 minutes before using to give the flours some time to hydrate.

Use a 1-ounce (28-gram) ladle to scoop batter onto the waffle iron and cook until crisp and lightly browned, 4 to 5 minutes (or follow the manufacturer's instructions). Finished waffles may be kept warm on a wire rack set over a baking sheet in a 200°F (95°C) oven while you prepare more. Extra waffles may be kept in an airtight container in the refrigerator for up to 5 days or frozen for up to a month and reheated in a toaster.

THE COMBINATION OF WHITE WHOLE WHEAT AND BARLEY FLOURS in these light whole-grain pancakes gives them a nutty flavor that pairs well with amber maple syrup. We've been known to substitute ground oats or cornmeal for the white whole wheat to make delicious variations. Add blueberries, raspberries, or even chocolate chips to the batter, if you like.

We've found that it's easiest to cook several pancakes at once on an electric griddle, which allows the cook to eat with everyone else. In fact, the electric griddle is a great piece of equipment for family meals, letting you make multiple grilled cheese sandwiches at once, heat hot dogs and buns at the same time, or reheat leftover pizza quickly and easily.

SERVES 3 OR 4

WHOLE-GRAIN PANCAKES

In a medium bowl, whisk together the white whole wheat flour, barley flour, salt, baking powder, and baking soda. In a separate bowl, whisk together the brown sugar, eggs, and buttermilk. Add the buttermilk mixture to the flour mixture and stir together with a rubber spatula until almost fully mixed. Add the melted butter and stir until the batter is smooth.

Heat an electric griddle to 325°F (165°C) or a heavy skillet. Use a 2-ounce (60 ml) ladle to scoop the batter onto the griddle. Cook until the bottoms are set and bubbles appear on the surface of the batter, 2 to 3 minutes. Flip the pancakes and cook until they are a deep golden brown on both sides, 2 to 3 more minutes. Serve immediately with butter and maple syrup.

1 cup / 140 grams **white whole wheat flour**

1 cup / 140 grams **barley flour**

¾ teaspoon / 4.5 grams **fine sea salt**

1 teaspoon / 6 grams **baking powder**

½ teaspoon / 2.5 grams **baking soda**

2 tablespoons / 27 grams **light brown sugar**

2 large **eggs**

2 cups / 480 grams **cultured buttermilk,** homemade (page 54) or store-bought

2 tablespoons / 28 grams **unsalted butter,** melted, plus more for serving

Grade B maple syrup, for serving

WHITE WHOLE WHEAT FLOUR is milled from spring white wheat and is lighter in color and flavor than traditional whole wheat flour, which is milled from red wheat. It makes adding a little extra flavor and fiber into your baked goods easier and more delicious for people who aren't used to the stronger flavor and darker color of traditional whole wheat flours.

BISCUITS ARE THE ULTIMATE COMFORT FOOD, AND GLUTEN-FREE flour gives them an indefinable nutty, savory quality. The gluten-free flour also works beautifully for thickening, and it goes without saying that the better your sausage, the better your gravy. This is one of our all-time favorite breakfasts.

SERVES 8

GLUTEN-FREE BISCUITS & GRAVY

MAKE THE BISCUITS: Preheat the oven to 425°F (220°C).

In a medium bowl, whisk together the gluten-free flour, sugar, baking powder, baking soda, and salt until well blended. Drop the butter into the flour mixture and quickly rub it in with your fingertips until the mixture looks like coarse crumbs. Pour in the buttermilk and stir with a wooden spoon or spatula just until it comes together into a sticky dough. Turn the dough out onto a floured work surface. Dust the top of the dough with flour and fold and turn the dough a few times until it comes together. Pat it out to a thickness of about 1 inch (2.5 cm) and use a floured sharp round cutter to punch out 2-inch (5 cm) circles. The scraps can be re-formed and cut out one time.

Put the cut biscuits in a 9 × 13-inch (23 × 33 cm) baking dish, fitting them snugly together. Bake for 10 minutes, rotate the pan, and bake until the biscuits are golden brown and firm to the touch, 3 to 6 minutes more. Remove the pan from the oven and let the biscuits rest on the pan while you make the gravy.

MAKE THE GRAVY: Set a large heavy-bottomed pot over medium-high heat. Add the sausage and season with the garlic powder, cayenne, and salt. Cook the sausage, stirring and breaking it up with a silicone spatula, until browned, 8 to 10 minutes. Drain off the excess fat and add the flour. Cook over medium heat, stirring gently, for 2 to 3 minutes. Add the milk, bring the mixture to a simmer, and cook for 5 minutes to thicken the gravy. Serve with the biscuits.

BISCUITS

2½ cups / 300 grams **What IiF Gluten-Free Flour** (page 25)

2 tablespoons / 25 grams **sugar**

2½ teaspoons / 13 grams **baking powder**

½ teaspoon / 2.5 grams **baking soda**

1 teaspoon / 6 grams **fine sea salt**

8 tablespoons / 113 grams cold **unsalted butter,** cut into cubes

⅔ cup / 160 grams cold **cultured buttermilk,** homemade (page 54) or store-bought

GRAVY

1 pound / 450 grams **pork breakfast sausage,** bulk or links with casings removed

½ teaspoon / 1 gram **garlic powder**

¼ teaspoon / 0.5 gram **cayenne pepper**

½ teaspoon / 3 grams **fine sea salt**

6 tablespoons / 55 grams **What IiF Gluten-Free Flour** (page 25)

3 cups / 780 grams **whole milk**

GLUTEN-FREE FLOUR MIXES

Gluten-free foods are popping up everywhere. We think that everyone knows someone who has a gluten intolerance or celiac disease. Special diets are nothing unusual these days, and a good host or chef knows how to work around them. Years ago we had a gluten-free client for whom we catered. At that time we played with some of the commercial gluten-free flours but were unhappy with the flavor. As a result we simply eliminated flour-based recipes from his menus. Fast-forward several years and gluten-free diets have become almost commonplace. This made us realize that gluten-free flour was something we needed to take a serious look at.

There is an abundance of them on the market, but they are expensive. We felt sure that we could make something better at home. Then Thomas Keller came out with his gluten-free flour, C4C (Cup4Cup). This made us take notice, because if Thomas Keller was putting his name on something, then it had to work. Never able to resist a challenge, Alex took a look at the ingredient list and set about developing his own version. We called the first version What IiF flour, for Ideas in Food. Then we considered the fact that corn allergies and xanthan sensitivities are often seen in people with gluten sensitivities, so we kept tinkering. The result is our Batch 2 flour, which is a slightly nuttier, more flavorful rendition of our original gluten-free flour and doesn't contain any corn products. We've found that both flours are easily substituted for all-purpose flour at a 1:1 ratio by weight. We've happily included the recipes for them here so that you can make and use them in your kitchens. The recipes for both are by weight only, because accuracy is very important to the blending process.

NOTE: If the nonfat dry milk is smooth and not clumpy, you can eliminate the blender step and thoroughly whisk everything together. Organic Valley nonfat dry milk is perfect for these recipes.

WHAT IIF GLUTEN-FREE FLOUR

MAKES 16¾ CUPS / 2,020 GRAMS

700 grams **cornstarch**

450 grams **tapioca starch**

450 grams **white rice flour**

200 grams **brown rice flour**

200 grams **nonfat dry milk**

20 grams **xanthan gum**

In a large bowl, whisk together the cornstarch, tapioca starch, white rice flour, brown rice flour, dry milk, and xanthan gum. In small batches, transfer the mixture to a blender, filling the blender about halfway. Turn the blender on low and then increase the speed to high to pulverize any lumps in the powders and uniformly blend them together. Combine the batches in a large bowl. Once everything has been blended, whisk the mixture well before transferring the flour into zip-top bags. It will keep for up to a year. This flour can be substituted for wheat flours in equal amounts by weight in recipes.

BATCH 2 GLUTEN-FREE FLOUR

MAKES 16¾ CUPS / 2,020 GRAMS

350 grams **arrowroot powder**

350 grams **sorghum flour**

450 grams **tapioca starch**

450 grams **white rice flour or millet flour**

200 grams **brown rice flour (or additional sorghum flour)**

200 grams **nonfat dry milk**

20 grams **guar gum**

In a large bowl, whisk together the arrowroot, sorghum flour, tapioca starch, white rice flour, brown rice flour, dry milk, and guar gum. In small batches, transfer the mixture to a blender, filling the blender about halfway. Turn the blender on low and then increase the speed to high to pulverize any lumps in the powders and uniformly blend them together. Combine the batches in a large bowl. Once everything has been blended, whisk the mixture well before transferring the flour into zip-top bags. It will keep for up to a year. This flour can be substituted for wheat flours in equal amounts by weight in recipes.

THIS IS A FUN SPIN ON THE CLASSIC SHRIMP AND GRITS. WE make an easy and flavorful sausage with the shrimp. Grinding the shrimp with the seasonings and then letting the mixture marinate before cooking allows the spices to permeate the shrimp gently without overpowering its delicate flavor. We use a pressure cooker to cook the grits because it cooks them quickly and evenly, and you can put everything in the bowl of the cooker and refrigerate it the evening before, letting the grits soak overnight. Then you just turn the pressure cooker on when you make your morning coffee. This meal is easy to pull together first thing in the morning and so good that no one will guess how little time it took.

SERVES 8

POACHED EGGS & SHRIMP GRITS

MAKE THE SAUSAGE: The day before serving, in a medium bowl, toss together the shrimp, wine, parsley, lemon zest, fennel seeds, onion powder, garlic powder, and pepper flakes. Grind in a meat grinder through the ¼-inch (6 mm) die. Alternatively, you can pulse the mixture in a food processor until minced. Gently mix the ground shrimp to make sure it is evenly combined and then put it in a large zip-top bag. Refrigerate for at least 4 hours and up to 12 hours.

MAKE THE GRITS: Put 2 inches (5 cm) of water in the bottom of a pressure cooker and set a small rack in the bottom. Put the grits, water, skim milk, buttermilk, hot sauce, and salt in a bowl that will easily fit inside the cooker and stir to combine. Set the bowl on the rack and cook at high pressure for 10 minutes. Let the pressure dissipate naturally.

(recipe continues)

SHRIMP SAUSAGE

2 pounds / 900 grams **shrimp,** peeled and deveined

¼ cup / 55 grams **dry white wine**

1½ cups / 28 grams fresh **parsley leaves**

Grated zest of 3 **lemons**

1½ tablespoons / 8 grams **fennel seeds**

1½ teaspoons / 3 grams **onion powder**

1½ teaspoons / 3 grams **garlic powder**

1 teaspoon / 2 grams **crushed red pepper flakes**

GRITS

1 cup plus 2 tablespoons / 200 grams **coarse ground grits**

1⅔ cups / 375 grams **water**

¾ cup plus 2 tablespoons / 200 grams **skim milk**

¾ cup plus 2 tablespoons / 200 grams **cultured buttermilk,** homemade (page 54) or store-bought

2 teaspoons / 10 grams **hot sauce,** preferably Crystal

1 teaspoon / 6 grams **fine sea salt**

POACH THE EGGS: Meanwhile, set a large pot of water with a generous splash of white vinegar over high heat. Once the water has come to a rolling boil, crack the eggs into a small bowl. Stir the water with a slotted spoon as you slide the eggs from the bowl into the water one by one. Turn the heat down to medium as the eggs slowly begin to coagulate in the pot. Do not let the water rise above a simmer. Cook until the whites are set and the yolks are still soft, 3 to 4 minutes, and then use a slotted spoon to transfer the eggs to a plate lined with a clean kitchen towel. Pat them dry with the edge of the towel or with a clean paper towel.

Set a large skillet over medium heat. Add the olive oil and, once it begins to shimmer, add the shrimp sausage. Cook the sausage slowly, turning and folding the mixture so that chunks of various sizes form, until lightly browned, 5 to 8 minutes. Remove the pan from the heat. Sprinkle with the scallions and stir gently to blend.

Open the pressure cooker—the grits may look separated and curdled, but just stir them with a silicone spatula and they will smooth out and become creamy. Spoon the grits into each of 8 bowls. Spoon the shrimp sausage over the grits and top with a poached egg. Season the egg with salt and pepper and serve immediately.

EGGS

Distilled white vinegar

8 large cold **eggs**

2 tablespoons / 28 grams **olive oil**

1 bunch **scallions**, green parts only, thinly sliced

Fine sea salt and **freshly ground black pepper**

UNDER PRESSURE

It's no secret that we love the pressure cooker. It's probably the most efficient cooking tool available. We prefer the electric cooker because it is quieter, has its own timer, and is easier to clean, but whichever one you choose—electric or stovetop—you'll be happy to have it in your kitchen. The days of exploding pressure cookers are long gone, as modern versions have several built-in safety measures to keep you safe in your kitchen, so there's no reason why you shouldn't get one of these amazing pieces of equipment.

Here's a brief primer for those who don't know how a pressure cooker works. As liquid boils inside it, steam is created. The steam builds up inside the chamber and exerts a uniform pressure on the ingredients inside. This pressure causes the temperature of the steam to increase. The increase in temperature is directly proportional to the amount of pressure, which is why most cookers have two settings, high and low pressure. Food cooks more quickly at high pressure. It's worth noting that when using a pressure cooker, cooking times start once the cooker has reached full pressure, not from the time you turn on the heat. Additionally, unless you release the pressure manually, there is a cooling-down period as the pressure slowly dissipates inside the machine.

The pressure cooker creates a very moist environment inside the chamber, making it a great alternative for braises. Moist heat is wonderful for breaking down connective tissue and extracting gelatin. Starches and legumes also do very well in the pressure cooker, cooking much more quickly and uniformly than they do on top of the stove. We do a 5-minute low-pressure cook in plain water with kombu to take the place of presoaking, and then we pressure-cook our beans in seasoned liquid for anywhere from 10 to 45 minutes, depending on the size of the bean and the preparation. Cooking beans in a traditional fashion would take more than a day, so pressure-cooking greatly speeds up the process.

Coarse grits and hearty grains also cook in a fraction of the time in a pressure cooker versus regular cooking, and with no danger of scorching or boiling over. A 6-quart pressure cooker is the perfect size for small batches of stock made from the bones of last night's dinner, or a batch of soup or chili for a last-minute dinner. The steam penetrates the food and the aromatics are contained in the chamber, creating a more flavorful end product. What's not to love about that?

THOUGH OFTEN MALIGNED, THE MICROWAVE IS A GREAT PIECE of equipment that most of us have in our kitchens. Microwaves work by emitting radio waves that enter the food and interact with water, fats, and sugars, causing them to vibrate and creating heat in the food. Thicker, denser foods cook more unevenly because it's harder for the microwaves to penetrate their interiors. Microwaves still cook more evenly than conventional ovens because the heat can be generated throughout the food instead of having to work its way from the outside in. We aerate the batter for these "Danishes" using an iSi whipped cream dispenser, and the batter expands easily in the microwave, creating a spongelike appearance and incredibly light texture while still retaining the creamy cheese flavor of an actual Danish. We like to pair them with fresh berries because the contrast of their sweet tart flavor and firmer texture helps bring out the ethereal qualities of these wonderful little cakes.

MAKES ABOUT 12 CAKES

MICROWAVE CHEESE "DANISH"

9 tablespoons plus 1 teaspoon / 150 grams **whole milk**

5 tablespoons plus 2 teaspoons / 24 grams **egg white powder**

7 ounces / 200 grams **cream cheese**

¼ cup / 75 grams **Lyle's Golden Syrup**

1 tablespoon plus 2 teaspoons / 25 grams **all-purpose flour**

¼ teaspoon / 1.5 grams **fine sea salt**

¼ cup / 10 grams finely ground **freeze-dried strawberries,** for dusting the cakes (optional)

Put the milk in a blender and turn it on low speed. Sprinkle in the egg white powder and increase the speed to medium. Puree the mixture for 15 seconds. Turn off the blender and add the cream cheese, syrup, flour, and salt. Turn the speed to high and puree until smooth, at least 30 seconds.

Pour the batter into the 1-liter canister of an iSi whipped cream dispenser and put the lid on. Charge with one N_2O charger and then shake to distribute the gas and allow it to be absorbed into the batter. Repeat with a second charger. The batter should feel and sound fluid in the canister. Take twelve 8-ounce (240 ml) paper cups and use the tip of a paring knife to make a slit in the bottom of each cup and 3 slits around the sides to let steam vent as the danishes cook. The batter will be thick enough to not leak through. Dispense the batter into the paper cups, filling each halfway. Working with one at a time, microwave on high for 30 seconds. Immediately remove the cup from the microwave and invert it (with the cake still in it) and set it on a plate or tray to keep the cakes from falling as they cool.

Once all the cakes are cooked, refrigerate the cups (still inverted) for at least 1 hour, until they are fully chilled and set. Use a paring knife to loosen the edges of each cold "Danish" from its cup and shake it free. Use a small fine-mesh sieve to dust the cakes with freeze-dried strawberry powder, if desired, and serve immediately.

USING AN ISI WHIPPED CREAM DISPENSER TO FILL PAPER CUPS WITH BATTER

JUST-BAKED
MICROWAVE
CHEESE "DANISH"

STRAWBERRY
POWDER-DUSTED
"DANISHES"

INSPIRED BY THE GREAT ST. LOUIS GOOEY BUTTER CAKE, THIS recipe has a gooey layer to go underneath the streusel on an otherwise classic coffee cake. The flavor of the sourdough gives a wonderful tanginess that balances the sugar.

If you want to change things up, you could add up to a cup of chopped fruit between the gooey and streusel layers or add up to a teaspoon of your favorite sweet spices like cinnamon, ginger, nutmeg, or clove to the batter in the initial beating stage. Whole grain devotees may want to substitute up to 1 cup of whole-grain flour for the all-purpose—or you could go whole hog and use 100 percent white whole wheat flour (just remember to increase the baking powder by ½ teaspoon/3 grams if you go that route). Another variation we love is to substitute ½ cup (43 grams) cocoa powder (we like King Arthur Double-Dutch Dark) for flour to make a chocolate sourdough cake—and/or you can add 1 cup (170 grams) chocolate chips or 1 cup (150 grams) roasted nuts to the finished batter before you pour it into the cake pan. We love how versatile this recipe is!

One note: Remember to make the streusel topping before the gooey topping and cake batter because they all get layered together before the cake goes into the oven.

MAKES ONE 9-INCH / 23 CM
TUBE CAKE

GOOEY TOPPING

8 tablespoons / 113 grams **unsalted butter,** at room temperature

¼ cup packed / 50 grams **dark brown sugar**

1 cup / 200 grams **granulated sugar**

¼ teaspoon / 1.5 grams **fine sea salt**

1 large **egg yolk,** at room temperature

3 tablespoons / 56.25 grams **Lyle's Golden Syrup**

2 tablespoons / 28 grams **water**

½ teaspoon / 2 grams **vanilla extract**

1 cup / 150 grams **all-purpose flour**

SOURDOUGH COFFEE CAKE

MAKE THE GOOEY TOPPING: In a stand mixer fitted with the paddle attachment, beat the butter, sugars, and salt until light and fluffy, about 2 minutes. Add the egg yolk and mix until well blended. Add the syrup and mix on low speed until well blended, 1 to 2 minutes. Add the water and vanilla and mix until well blended. Add the flour and mix on low speed until it comes together as a homogeneous mixture, scraping down the bowl as needed, 1 to 2 minutes. Transfer to a lidded container or zip-top bag and store in the refrigerator for up to 2 weeks.

(recipe continues)

MAKE THE COFFEE CAKE: Preheat the oven to 350°F (175°C). Butter a 9-inch (23 cm) tube cake pan with a removable bottom and put it on a baking sheet lined with parchment paper.

In a stand mixer fitted with the paddle attachment, beat the butter, sugar, baking powder, and salt until the mixture is light and fluffy, 2 to 3 minutes. Increase the mixer speed to medium and add the eggs one at a time, beating well after each addition. Add the flour and mix until it is fully incorporated, 1 to 2 minutes. Turn the mixer off and add the milk and the sourdough starter. Turn the mixer on low speed, then turn it up to medium and mix until a smooth, silky batter is formed, 15 to 20 seconds.

Transfer the batter to the prepared cake pan, using a rubber spatula to smooth it into an even layer. Tap the pan on the table a few times to level it out and remove any air bubbles. Use a teaspoon to scoop dollops of the gooey topping all over the surface of the cake. Sprinkle the cake crumb streusel over the top.

Bake until the cake begins to pull away from the sides of the pan and the top feels firm when touched, or the internal temperature of the center of the cake registers 208°–210°F (97°–98°C), about 1 hour 20 minutes. Take the pan out of the oven and let the cake cool for 15 minutes in the pan. Then remove the sides and let the cake rest on a wire rack until cool, at least 1 hour.

COFFEE CAKE

8 tablespoons / 113 grams **unsalted butter,** at room temperature

1 cup / 200 grams **sugar**

2 teaspoons / 12 grams **baking powder**

½ teaspoon / 3 grams **fine sea salt**

2 large **eggs,** at room temperature

2 cups / 300 grams **all-purpose flour**

⅔ cup / 170 grams **whole milk,** at room temperature

1 cup / 200 grams **sourdough starter** (page 106)

Cake Crumb Streusel (recipe follows)

THE BEST WAY TO CHECK THE CAKE FOR DONENESS IS WITH A THERMOMETER.

CAKE CRUMB STREUSEL

We are a household of three, and sometimes cakes and cookies start to go stale before we can eat them all. We like to grind them up into crumbs, dry them out, and freeze them so that they aren't wasted. We often sprinkle the crunchy bits into ice cream, but when we find ourselves overloaded, we make cake crumb streusel. We use dry crumbs in the recipe below, but if you have fresh, moist crumbs, start with half the amount of butter and add the additional in tablespoons just until the mixture comes together.

1½ cups / 100 grams **dry cake crumbs**

⅔ cup / 100 grams **all-purpose flour**

6 tablespoons / 75 grams **sugar**

⅛ teaspoon / 0.75 gram **fine sea salt**

8 tablespoons / 113 grams **unsalted butter,** at room temperature, diced

In a food processor, combine the cake crumbs, flour, sugar, and salt and pulse a few times to blend. Add the butter and pulse until the mixture forms small clumps. Transfer the mixture to a lidded container and store in the refrigerator for up to 2 weeks.

ROASTING NUTS

Back in the day, culinary instructors used to teach that if you were using nuts in something that was going to be baked or roasted you didn't need to toast them in advance. Hogwash! Nuts taste better when they've been toasted, and even if you are cooking them a second time, they benefit from an initial flavor boost. We generally toast nuts in a 350°F (175°C) oven for 5 to 15 minutes, depending on the nut, until they are golden brown and fragrant. They cool quickly at room temperature and are ready to use in both sweet and savory recipes.

We were pretty happy with this technique until we tasted pastry chef Philip Speer's pecans at the StarChefs International Congress in 2011. They were out of this world—incredibly dark, crisp, and delicious. His recipe called for boiling the nuts in a brown sugar syrup for 2 hours and then frying them.

Although the memory of Philip's recipe sticks with us, the reality of his technique was not something we were ready to tackle in our home kitchen. Even the idea of having to keep an eye on a pot bubbling away for 2 hours was daunting. So we adapted the idea and came up with a slightly less time-consuming and equally delicious (in our opinion) universal recipe for roasting nuts.

We take equal weights of nuts, sugar, and water, add a pinch (technically 0.3%) of salt, and put everything in a pot set over medium heat. Then we bring the mixture to a boil and let it cook for 5 minutes to soften up the nuts so that the syrup can penetrate them. Remove the pan from the heat, cover, and steep for 20 minutes. Strain off and discard the syrup, and toss the nuts with a little butter and salt. The nuts are still warm enough to melt the butter, and it emulsifies with the syrup still clinging to them to form a thin glaze—and the cooler your nuts, the thicker the resulting glaze. We then roast them in the oven on a parchment paper–lined baking sheet until they are a deep golden brown, 10 to 20 minutes, depending on the type of nuts. Take the pan out of the oven and let cool completely.

Once cool, the nuts are crunchy, delicious, and only slightly sweet. You can add some fresh herbs or spices to the syrup, but don't expect to save that liquid. The sugar syrup pulls some of the tannins from the nuts, which makes them mellower with a pronounced nutty flavor, but the sugar syrup ends up tasting quite bitter.

BASIC ROASTED NUTS

About 1 cup / 150 grams **whole nuts**

¾ cup / 150 grams **sugar**

5 ounces / 150 grams **water**

⅜ teaspoon / 2.25 grams **fine sea salt**

2 teaspoons / 10 grams **unsalted butter**

This recipe can be multiplied to make as large a batch as you need. The important thing is that you use equal weights of nuts, sugar, and water as your starting point. We generally add ½ teaspoon of spices to the sugar syrup in the beginning to add any extra flavors. They will mostly be strained off with the syrup before roasting, so you need to make sure their flavor permeates the nuts. The cooking time below will result in a medium roast. If you are not cooking the nuts a second time (in a cake or something), try roasting them for an extra 5 to 10 minutes, until they are a deep mahogany, and see how rich the flavor becomes.

In a small saucepan, combine the nuts, sugar, water, and ¼ teaspoon (1.5 grams) of the salt. Bring the mixture to a boil over medium-high heat and simmer for 5 minutes. Remove the pan from the heat, cover, and let the nuts steep for 20 minutes.

Preheat the oven to 350°F (175°C). Line a baking sheet with parchment paper.

Strain the nuts, discarding the syrup, and transfer them to a medium bowl. Add the butter and remaining ⅛ teaspoon (0.75 gram) salt, and toss well. Spread the nuts out on the baking sheet. Roast for 10 to 15 minutes, rotating once, until the nuts are a deep golden brown. Let them cool completely—the nuts will crisp up as they cool down. Transfer them to an airtight container. The nuts will keep for up to 2 weeks in an airtight container at room temperature.

2

BREADS

WE USE CHOUX PASTE FOR THIS RECIPE BECAUSE IT PRODUCES delicate and airy popovers—and you can make the dough in advance. The make-ahead versatility of the popover technique is perfect for breakfast, too. Garlic bread popovers are delicious alongside crisp bacon and runny eggs; they are a great stand-in for classic Yorkshire puddings with a roast and a wonderful companion for thick stews or roasted fish. They go with everything because they are a striking combination of light, crisp, and flavorful.

MAKES ABOUT 24 POPOVERS

GARLIC BREAD POPOVERS

MAKE THE CHOUX PASTE: In a medium saucepan, combine the milk, garlic butter, and salt. Bring to a simmer over medium-high heat. Add the flours and stir until the dough forms a ball, pulling away from the edges and forming a light film on the bottom of the pan, 2 to 3 minutes. Transfer the dough to a stand mixer fitted with the paddle attachment. Mix the dough on medium-low for 5 minutes until it cools, and then start adding the eggs one at a time, allowing each one to be absorbed into the dough before adding the next. Add the cheese and mix until just combined. Turn off the mixer and set the bowl in an ice water bath for about 30 minutes until the dough is cool. Refrigerate it overnight in a covered container.

MAKE THE CHEESE TOPPING: In a medium bowl, stir together the flour, cheese, and salt. Use a rubber spatula to stir in the melted garlic butter. Transfer the cheese dough to a sheet of parchment paper and cover with another piece of parchment paper. Use a rolling pin to roll the dough out to a thickness of ⅛ inch (3 mm). Put the rolled-out dough onto a baking sheet and put it in the freezer. Let it freeze completely, about 45 minutes.

Remove the dough from the freezer and remove the top layer of parchment. Use a 1.5-inch (4 cm) round cutter to punch out the dough, making 24 pieces. Transfer the dough rounds to a plate, cover them with plastic wrap, and put in the refrigerator. The dough trimmings may be brought back to room temperature and rolled again one time if necessary.

(recipe continues)

CHOUX PASTE

1⅓ cups / 360 grams **whole milk**

6.25 ounces (12½ tablespoons) / 175 grams **Garlic Butter** (recipe follows)

1 teaspoon / 6 grams **fine sea salt**

1 cup / 150 grams **all-purpose flour**

⅔ cup / 100 grams **barley flour**

6 large **eggs**

2 cups / 150 grams freshly grated **Gruyère cheese,** plus more for serving

CHEESE TOPPING

⅔ cup / 100 grams **all-purpose flour**

1 cup / 100 grams freshly grated **Parmigiano Reggiano cheese**

¼ teaspoon / 1.5 grams **fine sea salt**

4 ounces (8 tablespoons) / 112 grams **Garlic Butter** (recipe follows), melted

Preheat the oven to 425°F (218°C).

Scoop ½ cup (100 grams) of choux paste into each cup of a standard-size nonstick muffin tin. You will need two pans if you are baking them all at once. Put one round of cheese topping on top of each scoop of dough and press it down to make sure it is centered and level. Put the popovers into the oven and bake for 15 minutes.

Rotate the pan, decrease the oven temperature to 350°F (180°C), and bake until they are fully puffed and golden brown, 30 minutes more. Remove the pan from the oven, turn the popovers out of the pan, and let them cool on a wire rack for 5 minutes. Use a rasp-style grater to grate cheese over the tops. Serve hot.

CHOUX PASTE is a classic French dough, most commonly associated with pastries like cream puffs and éclairs. It is a classic example of steam leavening, where the high water content of the dough causes it to puff dramatically in the oven before the proteins in the flour and the eggs set around the hollow center. It has a light, crispy exterior and a moist, tender interior. As long as you cook it long enough in the initial mixing process, you almost can't go wrong with it. In addition to baking, choux paste is often deep-fried into doughnuts, as with Mexican *churros*, for an incredibly crispy outside and a light as air crumb.

GARLIC BUTTER

MAKES ABOUT 10.5 OUNCES (21 TABLESPOONS) / 300 GRAMS

6 **garlic** cloves

10 ounces / 283 grams **unsalted butter,** diced

½ cup / 12 grams chopped fresh **parsley**

Peel the garlic and use a mandoline to thinly slice it, discarding the ends. Put the garlic slices and butter in a small saucepan. Put over medium heat to melt the butter, and continue to cook until the garlic is just softened, 3 to 5 minutes. Add the parsley and cook until it becomes bright green and fragrant, 1 to 2 minutes. Remove the pan from the heat and transfer the mixture to a heatproof container. Let cool, uncovered, for 30 minutes, then cover and refrigerate for up to 2 weeks.

WE DEVELOPED THIS VERSATILE RECIPE WHEN WE WERE

running a small hotel in Colorado. Every morning we served breakfast. We wanted to be able to make great baked goods for everyone who stayed with us. These scones can be made to suit almost any dietary strictures, even gluten-free if you substitute one of our gluten-free blends (page 25) for the flours. And they are delicious. One of our favorite variations is the combination of peanut butter and fresh strawberries. The process of mixing them in the food processor yields a very tender scone, light as a feather and practically melting in your mouth. It was one of the recipes our guests requested most. If you like a little more structure to your scones, just knead the dough a few times before folding in the fruit. It's that easy to change.

1½ cups / 225 grams **all-purpose flour**

1½ cups / 210 grams **white whole wheat flour**

½ cup / 100 grams **granulated sugar**

2 teaspoons / 12 grams **baking powder**

½ teaspoon / 2.5 grams **baking soda**

½ teaspoon / 3 grams **fine sea salt**

1 cup / 270 grams **nut butter** (peanut, cashew, almond, etc.), cold

1 cup / 260 grams **whole milk** (or substitute soy, almond, or rice milk)

¾ cup **fruit** (berries, raisins, diced bananas, etc.)

2 tablespoons / 25 grams **raw sugar**

MAKES 12 SMALL SCONES

NUT BUTTER SCONES

Preheat the oven to 400°F (205°C). Line a baking sheet with parchment paper.

In a food processor, combine the flours, granulated sugar, baking powder, baking soda, and salt and pulse a few times to blend. Add the nut butter and pulse to blend. The mixture should look coarse and granular. Add ¾ cup (195 grams) of the milk and pulse until the mixture begins to clump together. If it seems too dry, add the remaining milk, 2 tablespoons (32.5 grams) at a time, pulsing in between additions, until it begins to clump together and look like coarse streusel.

Turn the dough out onto a lightly floured countertop and scatter the fruit over the top. Use your hands and a bench scraper, if you have one, to gently fold the fruit into the dough, adding a bit of flour if the juices from the fruit make the dough too wet to hold together. It should just hold when you press the dough together. Form the dough into an 8-inch (20 cm) round and cut it into 12 equal wedges. Or you can shape it into two 4-inch (10 cm) rounds and cut each into 6 pieces.

Put the scones on the baking sheet. Sprinkle the tops with the raw sugar. Bake for 8 minutes, rotate the sheet, and bake until golden brown, 4 to 8 minutes more, checking after 4 minutes. Let the scones cool on the baking sheet for 5 minutes before serving.

DANISH DOUGH IS THE BEST POSSIBLE HYBRID OF PIE DOUGH
and yeasted dough, because it combines the crispness and
flakiness of butter pie dough with the softness and flavor
of a slow-fermented yeast dough. It is traditionally made
using a technique known as lamination. Typically, to make a
lamination, you take yeasted dough and a butter block, wrap
the dough around the butter, and then carefully fold it to create
several hundred layers. When you bake the dough it becomes
incredibly light and flaky from the combination of yeast and
steam leavening. The action of the yeast makes the dough rise
as it bakes, while the steam leavening that occurs when water
evaporates out of the butter creates the honeycomb structure
that is the hallmark of laminated pastries.

This version takes a different approach. We cut the butter
into the flour mixture as we would for pie dough, and keep the
traditional turns, or folding, of the dough in order to create
layers of butter and flour in the finished dough. It's a little less
finicky than the original, and the long fermentation ensures a
great yeasty flavor in the finished Danish.

MAKES 16 PASTRIES

NO-KNEAD DANISH

DOUGH

4⅔ cups / 700 grams **all-purpose flour**

12 ounces / 340 grams cold **unsalted butter,** cut into slices

1¼ teaspoons / 3.5 grams **instant yeast**

6½ tablespoons / 80 grams **sugar**

2½ teaspoons / 15 grams **fine sea salt**

1½ cups / 405 grams **whole milk,** at room temperature

2 large **eggs,** at room temperature

2 tablespoons / 28 grams **unsalted butter,** melted and cooled

MAKE THE DOUGH: Put 2 cups (300 grams) of the flour in a food processor
and add the butter. Pulse until the butter and flour become evenly
combined into a coarse, slightly chunky meal.

Put the remaining 2⅔ cups (400 grams) of flour in a large bowl.
Add the yeast, sugar, and salt to the bowl and whisk together. Stir the
butter-flour mixture into the dry ingredients. In a separate medium
bowl, whisk together the milk, eggs, and melted butter. Pour the wet
ingredients into the bowl of dry ingredients and use a wooden spoon to
stir the mixture until it is completely combined into a damp, shaggy ball.

(recipe continues)

Cover the bowl with plastic wrap and let the dough rest at a warm room temperature of 70°F (21°C) for 8 hours. Have faith at this point; it will come together nicely as it rises.

Uncover the bowl and use a rubber spatula to gently loosen the dough from the bowl. Dampen your hands with cool water and slide one hand under one side of the dough. Fold that side of the dough into the center and press it down gently so it adheres to itself. Give the bowl a quarter turn and repeat the folding process two more times. After the fourth fold, flip the dough over so the seams are on the bottom. Cover the bowl with plastic wrap and let the dough rise at room temperature for 10 to 12 hours. (We usually let it go overnight.)

After the dough has risen, repeat the 4 folds from the previous step, and then transfer the dough to a large parchment paper—lined baking sheet. Gently press the dough out on the parchment paper so that it is almost the same size as the pan. Cover the dough with plastic wrap and refrigerate for 3 hours.

Remove the dough from the refrigerator. Liberally dust a countertop or cutting board with flour and transfer the dough to the floured surface. Roll the dough into a large rectangle that is about ½ inch (13 mm) thick, using just enough extra flour to keep it from sticking. Fold the two outside sections inward to meet in the center of the dough. Gently shape the dough so that the layers sit evenly and the entire thing forms a new rectangle that is half as wide as the original. Use your rolling pin to gently roll the dough out to a thickness of ¼ inch (6 mm), being careful to keep the layers together and the shape of the rectangle. Position the dough so that it is taller than it is wide. Fold the top third of the dough down to cover the middle third of the dough, and then fold the bottom third of the dough up over those 2 layers, as if you were folding a letter to be put in an envelope. If the edges of the rectangle are uneven, use a sharp knife to trim them in a straight line. If the dough is too soft to cut evenly, wait until after you have chilled the dough for the next step before trimming.

Put the dough onto the prepared baking sheet and cover with plastic wrap. Put the dough in the refrigerator to chill for at least 1 hour and no more than 3 hours. Remove the dough from the refrigerator and roll the dough out into a rectangle ½ inch (13 mm) thick and repeat the tri-fold process described above. Refrigerate for at least 1 hour and no more than 3 hours and then repeat the folding process one more time. After the last fold, put the dough back onto the baking sheet, cover with plastic wrap, and refrigerate overnight.

From top: ROLLING THE DOUGH; FOLDING THE DOUGH; THE FINISHED ROLLED AND FOLDED DOUGH

MAKE THE FILLING: In a medium bowl, whisk together the cream cheese, sugar, egg yolk, salt, and mace. Use immediately or put the mixture in a covered container and refrigerate until ready to use, up to 2 days.

When ready to make the Danish, put the filling in a pastry bag fitted with a ½-inch (13 mm) plain tip. Remove the dough from the refrigerator. Cut the dough in half, put the other half back on the baking sheet, cover with plastic wrap, and return it to the refrigerator. Lightly flour a countertop or cutting board and roll the dough out into a 10 × 18-inch (25 × 46 cm) rectangle. Pipe two lines of filling, side by side, across the length of the dough, from edge to edge, and about 3 inches (8 cm) up from the bottom of the dough. Fold the bottom of the dough up over the filling and continue to roll the dough into a log, as if you were making cinnamon rolls. Cut the log of dough crosswise into 8 equal pieces and arrange them on a parchment paper–lined baking sheet in a 2 by 4 grid. Cover loosely with plastic wrap and repeat the process with the other half of the dough and a second baking sheet. Let both sheets of Danish proof at room temperature for 1 hour, until they have risen and look puffy and marshmallow-like.

Preheat the oven to 380°F (195°C).

In a small bowl, mix the crème fraîche and egg yolks with a pastry brush until they are well blended. Brush each Danish with the egg wash twice. Sprinkle with the raw sugar. Bake the Danish for 20 minutes, rotate the pans, turning them from front to back and switching racks from top to bottom, and bake until they are a deep golden brown, 10 more minutes more. Transfer the Danish to racks to cool for 10 minutes. Serve warm.

FILLING

8 ounces / 225 grams **cream cheese**

¼ cup / 50 grams **sugar**

1 large **egg yolk**

Very scant ¼ teaspoon / 1 gram **fine sea salt**

⅛ teaspoon / 0.25 gram **ground mace**

3 tablespoons / 45 grams **crème fraîche**, homemade (page 55) or store-bought, or heavy cream

2 large **egg yolks**

¼ cup / 50 grams **raw sugar**

RAW SUGAR, or turbinado sugar, is made from unrefined sugarcane juice, so it may contain trace minerals and nutrients. The reason we like raw sugar is because it generally has a coarse texture and doesn't melt as easily as granulated or brown sugars. This means that when you sprinkle it on baked goods before baking, you get a nice crunchy top on the finished sweets. It also gives crumbles and streusel toppings an unexpected texture and soft crunch that is very appealing.

CURDS & WHEY

We love to cook with buttermilk, crème fraîche, ricotta, and cream cheese. In many cases culturing dairy products and making cheese at home will be less expensive and the results will taste better than what you can buy from a store. When we "culture" dairy products we introduce beneficial bacteria to the milk to jump-start the fermentation process, which changes the texture and flavor of the milk to create ingredients like crème fraîche, buttermilk, and various cheeses. It is so easy to make fresh cheeses at home—all it takes is time, heat, a thermometer, and a strainer.

These days natural buttermilk, a by-product of the butter-making process, is hard to come by unless you churn your own butter. Cultured buttermilk is the kind we buy at supermarkets and farmers' markets and is usually referred to as simply "buttermilk." It adds the same creamy dairy effect as milk in recipes, with the added benefit of a hint of acid to balance the flavors. When you make it at home you can use whole milk, which results in buttermilk so thick you can practically spoon it out of the container.

Cultured dairy products, either homemade or store-bought, can be used as a starter to make other cultured dairy products. For example, we add buttermilk to cream to make crème fraîche—an ingredient notable for its rich texture and the fact that it doesn't curdle when you cook with it. If you let your crème fraîche sit out at room temperature for a day or two, it will separate, the thickened cream rising to the top of the container, leaving the whey on the bottom. When you spoon off the top layer you have something closer to American sour cream, which is thicker and creamier than traditional French crème fraîche. Either version can be used to make cultured butter in the recipe opposite.

Buttermilk that is allowed to sit out at room temperature for 1 to 3 days will also separate. The top layer is a delicious uncooked cream cheese, which can be seasoned to your taste and used as traditional store-bought cream cheese. The type of milk you use to make your buttermilk will dictate how much fat is in the finished cheese. It is tangy and smooth and has a wonderful fresh flavor.

A by-product of playing with dairy fermentation at home is the whey. Cultured whey is unbeatable for the home pickling process. Pickles are a product of lactic fermentation, and adding whey to your pickling liquid makes a huge difference in both the speed of fermentation and the quality of the finished product. The less time it takes for your pickles to ferment, the fresher and crisper the finished pickles. Whey is also a stellar cooking ingredient. We use it for marinades and brines and for cooking grains and beans. We also infuse it with spices and use it to poach fruit. It has a gentle tartness and an inherent sweetness that make for a wonderful background note in many savory and sweet preparations.

All of the recipes in the book will work with store-bought dairy products, but in the interest of flavor, we wanted to give you a few good recipes for making your own.

BUTTER & NATURAL BUTTERMILK

MAKES ABOUT 8 OUNCES / 226 GRAMS BUTTER
AND 3 CUPS / 720 GRAMS BUTTERMILK

1 quart / 960 grams **heavy cream** or crème fraîche

You can make this butter with either heavy cream or crème fraîche. If you are an adventurous cook, we suggest that you try making both kinds and then doing a side-by-side comparison so that you taste the difference that fermentation makes. You may be surprised by how thin the buttermilk is. That's because almost all of the buttermilk that you buy from a store is cultured buttermilk. Buttermilk that comes from cultured butter, despite the difference in texture, can be used in the same way as any other cultured buttermilk.

Let the cream sit out at room temperature for about 1 hour to warm up to about 50°F (10°C). Put the cream in a food processor and let it run continuously until it whips into firm peaks. At this point, pulse the food processor until the whipped cream separates into butter and buttermilk, 3 to 5 minutes. The butter will form small granules floating in a milky liquid. Line a large strainer with damp cheesecloth and set the strainer over a large bowl. Pour the mixture into the strainer and let drain for about 10 minutes. Alternatively, you can refrigerate the butter in its liquid for up to 48 hours to allow the flavor to develop.

Once most of the liquid has drained off, twist the top of the cheesecloth to contain the butter and gently squeeze it over the strainer to remove excess buttermilk. Once it seems dry, take the butter (still in the cheesecloth) over to the sink and rinse it under cool, running water, squeezing it gently, to remove any remaining buttermilk. Transfer the butter to a cool cutting board or marble slab and knead gently with damp, cool hands until all of the buttermilk is expelled. Wrap the butter tightly in plastic wrap and refrigerate for up to 4 weeks. The buttermilk can be stored in a covered container in the refrigerator for up to 2 weeks.

CULTURED BUTTERMILK

MAKES 1 QUART / 900 GRAMS

1 quart / 1,040 grams **whole or low-fat milk**

¼ cup / 60 grams **cultured buttermilk, homemade or store-bought**

Cultured buttermilk, the kind normally found in supermarkets, is thicker and creamier than natural buttermilk and it can be made from whole or low-fat milk because the texture is more directly a result of the fermentation process than of the fat content.

Pour the milk into a generous quart container and add the buttermilk. Close the lid and shake to blend. If your container holds exactly a quart, omit ¼ cup (65 grams) of the milk. Leave the container out at room temperature for 24 to 48 hours until it has thickened. Store the finished buttermilk in a covered container in the refrigerator for up to 2 weeks. The finished buttermilk can be used to culture the next batch.

RICOTTA

MAKES 1 GENEROUS QUART / 1,000 GRAMS

6 cups / 1,560 grams **whole milk**

1 pint / 480 grams **cultured buttermilk, homemade (above) or store-bought**

3 cups / 720 grams **heavy cream**

This recipe uses the acid from the buttermilk to coagulate the cheese. You will find that the gentle lactic acids and the combination of milk and heavy cream transform your basic ricotta into a true delicacy to be savored and enjoyed.

In a large saucepan, combine the milk, buttermilk, and cream. Set over medium heat and stir to blend in the beginning and then do not stir again. Bring the mixture to 190°F (88°C); do not overheat the mixture. Remove the pan from the heat. Cover the pot and let it sit at room temperature until cool, 5 to 6 hours.

Line a large strainer with damp cheesecloth and set the strainer over a bowl. Ladle the ricotta cheese into the strainer and let drain for about 1 hour. The ricotta and the whey can be stored in separate covered containers in the refrigerator for up to 2 weeks.

FRESH CREAM CHEESE

1 quart / 960 grams **cultured buttermilk,** homemade (opposite) or store-bought

Fine sea salt (optional)

One of the by-products of this naturally fermented cream cheese is whey. Whey is also found in many store-bought products like yogurt and sour cream. It is the clear liquid that separates out in the container. It is used to jump-start lactic fermentation in pickles and in recipes for cooking grains and beans as a flavorful replacement for some of the water.

Put the buttermilk in a covered container and let sit at room temperature for 2 to 3 days. The curds and whey will separate and a layer of whey will appear at the bottom of the container.

Line a large strainer with damp cheesecloth and set the strainer over a bowl. Put the buttermilk in the cheesecloth and let drain for 3 to 4 hours until all of the whey has drained off the cheese. Transfer any whey to a covered container. Twist the top of the cheesecloth closed over the cream cheese and tie it to a long wooden spoon set over the top of the strainer so that it hangs slightly above the strainer, using its weight to help it drain. Refrigerate for 8 hours. Transfer any whey to your container, and put the cream cheese in a covered container in the refrigerator. If you like, you may season the cream cheese with salt (0.3%) at this point. Both the cream cheese and the whey can be kept in separate, covered containers in the refrigerator for up to 2 weeks.

CRÈME FRAÎCHE

1 pint / 480 grams **heavy cream**

¼ cup / 60 grams **cultured buttermilk,** homemade (opposite) or store-bought

Put the cream and buttermilk in a pint container, close the lid, and shake to blend. If your container holds exactly 1 pint, omit ¼ cup (65 grams) of the cream. Leave the covered container out at room temperature for 24 to 48 hours until it has thickened to the desired consistency. Store in a covered container in the refrigerator for up to 2 weeks.

DEVELOPING THIS RECIPE WAS AN EXERCISE IN FRUSTRATION.
In order to get the coveted honeycomb structure inside the bread, you need wet, floppy dough that is hard to cut out and control. The key here is to wet both your hands and the cutter when you're working with the dough. Using semolina to dust the outsides instead of the classic cornmeal lets you reroll the scraps one time without destroying the texture of the inner crumb. Once mastered, homemade English muffins are easy. To get perfectly round muffins, you can buy English muffin rings; we use flan rings that we already own. You can also make these free-form; the irregular shapes give the muffins character. If using rings, remember to grease the inside and not to overfill them or it can be difficult to remove the bread after cooking. One final step to success is to be sure that your griddle is not too hot. We flip our muffins regularly to ensure even cooking throughout. A lower temperature is essential to making sure the insides are fully cooked before the outsides burn.

MAKES ABOUT 12 MUFFINS

ENGLISH MUFFINS

MAKE THE SPONGE: In a small bowl, combine the flour, water, and yeast. Stir to blend into a smooth mixture. Cover loosely with plastic wrap and let sit at room temperature for 3 to 4 hours, until the mixture is bubbly and has doubled its original volume.

MAKE THE ENGLISH MUFFINS: In a large bowl, combine the flour, yeast, salt, and sugar and whisk to blend thoroughly. Add the sponge, the sourdough starter, and water and stir with a rubber spatula or wooden spoon until everything is well blended and there are no lumps of flour. Cover the bowl with plastic wrap and leave at room temperature for 4 hours.

Remove the plastic wrap. Gently loosen the dough from the bowl. Slide a bench scraper or plastic spatula under one side of the dough. Fold that side of the dough into the center and press it down gently so it adheres to itself. Give the bowl a quarter turn and repeat the folding

(recipe continues)

SPONGE

1⅓ cups / 200 grams **all-purpose flour**

7 ounces / 200 grams **water**

1 teaspoon / 3 grams **instant yeast**

ENGLISH MUFFINS

5 cups / 750 grams **all-purpose flour**

½ teaspoon / 1.5 grams **instant yeast**

1 tablespoon / 18 grams **fine sea salt**

1 tablespoon / 12 grams **sugar**

About ½ cup / 90 grams **sourdough starter** (page 106)

3 cups / 675 grams **water**

Semolina, for dusting

process 3 more times. After the fourth fold, flip over the dough so the seams are on the bottom. Cover the bowl with plastic wrap and let the dough rest in the refrigerator for at least 6 and up to 12 hours, until you are ready to make English muffins.

Set a large sauté pan or griddle over medium-low heat, or preheat an electric griddle to 325°F (165°C).

Gently loosen the dough from the bowl and then turn it out onto a counter that has been generously dusted with semolina. Sprinkle the top with more semolina and wet your hands with cool water. Gently press out the dough to a thickness of ½ inch (13 mm), rewetting your hands as needed. Sprinkle the top with more semolina and then use a 3-inch (8 cm) round cutter, dipped in water, to cut out your muffins. Remove the scraps and set them aside. The dough may be pressed together and rerolled one time.

Coat your pan or griddle lightly with cooking spray and slide 4 muffins into the pan to cook. If you are using muffin rings, make sure they have been lightly greased on the inside and put one around each muffin as soon as you put them in the pan. Cook until they are golden brown on the bottom, about 5 minutes. Flip them over, still inside the rings, if using, and cook until they are golden brown on the second side, about 5 minutes. If they are still soft in the center, continue to cook the muffins, flipping them every 2 minutes or so until they are cooked through. This may take up to 12 minutes more. Transfer the muffins to a wire rack to cool completely. If the muffins are browning too quickly you can finish them in a low oven (200°F/95°C) until they are cooked through. Let the muffins cool completely before cutting or breaking them open to toast.

THE DOUGH AFTER 12 HOURS IN THE REFRIGERATOR

A SPONGE—which is what gets made in step 1 of this recipe—is used to give breads additional flavor. Also known as a biga, a poolish, or a pre-ferment, it is usually made of equal parts flour and water with a bit of commercial yeast. This soupy mixture is left to ferment at room temperature for at least 2 hours and up to 18 to activate the yeast and develop flavor before being added to dough. It is often used in combination with sourdough starters to help develop lighter breads with a bit less acidity and a thinner crust.

PARSNIPS HAVE A SWEET, EARTHY FLAVOR. LOOK FOR ONES that aren't too big, because large cores can get tough and woody. This great quick bread is perfect at breakfast time with cream cheese or in the afternoon with a cup of tea. The recipe makes two loaves and you can easily freeze one.

MAKES TWO 9 × 5-INCH /
23 × 13 CM LOAVES

PARSNIP-PEAR QUICK BREAD

Preheat the oven to 350°F (175°C). Butter and flour two 9 × 5-inch (23 × 13 cm) loaf pans.

Wash the parsnips and cut off the tips and stem ends. Peel the parsnips and put the peels into a small saucepan. Add the rice bran oil and set the pan over medium heat. Cook the peels until they turn golden brown, about 15 minutes. Remove the pan from the heat and cool to room temperature.

Meanwhile, use the large holes on a box grater to grate the parsnips until you have 4 cups (330 grams) of grated vegetable. Peel the pears and grate them as well.

In a large bowl, whisk together the eggs, sugar, and vanilla. Add the fried peels and the cooled parsnip oil and whisk to combine. Add the grated parsnips and pears and stir with a rubber spatula.

In a separate large bowl, whisk together the flours, cloves, cardamom, lemon zest, baking soda, baking powder, and salt. Add the hazelnuts and dried pears and stir with a rubber spatula to combine. Pour the egg mixture into the flour mixture and stir until just combined. Divide the batter evenly between the prepared pans. Bake the loaves on the middle rack of the oven for 45 minutes. Rotate the pans from front to back and bake until a cake tester inserted in the center comes out clean and the internal temperature of the loaves registers 205°–210°F (96°–98°C), about 25 minutes (a total of 1 hour 10 minutes). Let the bread cool for 20 minutes in the pans. Turn them out onto wire racks and let cool completely before serving.

2 pounds / 907 grams **parsnips**

1 cup / 225 grams **rice bran oil** or canola oil

¾ pound / 340 grams **red Anjou pears** (about 2)

3 large **eggs**

12 ounces / 350 grams **palm sugar,** grated on a box grater, or 1¾ cups packed dark brown sugar

2 teaspoons / 8 grams **vanilla extract**

2 cups / 300 grams **all-purpose flour**

1 cup / 140 grams **whole wheat flour**

¹⁄₁₆ teaspoon / 0.15 gram **ground cloves**

⅛ teaspoon / 0.25 gram **ground cardamom**

Grated zest of 1 **lemon**

1 teaspoon / 5 grams **baking soda**

½ teaspoon / 3 grams **baking powder**

1 teaspoon / 6 grams **fine sea salt**

¾ cup plus 2 tablespoons / 150 grams **hazelnuts,** roasted (see page 39)

⅓ cup / 65 grams **dried pears,** chopped

SOUPS
& STEWS

A NEAT PLAY ON GAZPACHO, THIS "SOUP" IS FROZEN AND SHAVED for serving, creating an incredibly light texture that slowly melts down into a smooth, cold soup in your mouth. It is refreshing on a hot summer day, a gazpacho version 2.0, if you will. Note that you'll need three ice cube trays to accomplish the freezing.

Almost all herbs flower in the summertime and we've added these small blossoms to the soup for great intense bursts of flavor. We are particularly fond of chive, basil, and thyme blossoms, which are usually abundant in our garden and herb pots. You can also sprinkle thinly sliced herbs over the top of the shaved ice, if you can't find blossoms.

SERVES 8

GREEN GAZPACHO

In a large bowl, combine the pistachios, grapes, melon, tomatillos, cucumbers, scallions, jalapeño, and salt and mix well. Divide the mixture between 2 gallon-size zip-top bags and make sure they are securely closed. Lay the bags out flat, one on top of the other, on a tray or baking sheet and put them in the freezer. Freeze until solid, at least 8 hours.

Transfer the bags to the refrigerator to let the mixture thaw, at least 12 hours. (If you are in a hurry, you can thaw them under cold running water for 1 hour.) The fruits and vegetables will soften and start releasing their liquid and this will help to get the most flavor out of them when you puree them. Transfer the contents of 1 bag to a large blender. Turn the blender on low speed and slowly increase the power to high speed, pureeing the mixture until completely smooth, 2 to 4 minutes. Strain the soup through a fine-mesh sieve into a large pitcher. Pour the soup into ice cube trays and put the trays in the freezer. Repeat with the second bag of soup. Freeze the soup in the ice cube trays until it is rock solid, at least 6 hours. At this point you can remove it from the trays and store the cubes in zip-top bags in the freezer for up to a week.

Chill a large metal bowl in the freezer for at least 1 hour before you are planning to serve the soup. Put 8 soup bowls into the refrigerator to chill. Set up a food processor with the thin slicing blade. Turn the food processor on and feed the frozen soup cubes through the feed tube and shave the soup. When the bowl of the food processor is halfway filled, stop the machine and transfer the shaved soup to the bowl in the freezer.

2 cups / 250 grams shelled **raw pistachios**

¾ pound / 340 grams **seedless green grapes** (about 1 bunch), stems removed

2 pounds / 930 grams **honeydew melon** (about 1), peeled, seeded, and cut into 1-inch / 2.5 cm chunks

¾ pound / 340 grams large **tomatillos** (4 to 5), husked and quartered

4 **baby cucumbers**, peeled and sliced

3 **scallions**, cut into 1-inch / 2.5 cm batons

1 **jalapeño**, peeled and sliced

1¾ teaspoons / 10.5 grams **fine sea salt**

About 3 tablespoons / 45 grams **pistachio oil**

Fleur de sel

Small handful of **herb flowers** or thinly sliced leaves

Repeat with the remaining soup. Grated gazpacho may be kept in the freezer for up to 1 hour.

To serve, put equal portions of the frozen, shaved gazpacho into each of the 8 chilled serving bowls. Drizzle about a teaspoon of pistachio oil over each serving and finish with a sprinkling of fleur de sel and a few assorted herb flowers.

CHINESE CELERY HAS LONG, SLENDER STALKS THAT ARE hollow and are topped with an abundance of soft green leaves. Stronger and more aromatic than the conventional celery we are all used to, it tends to have a slightly peppery flavor and is usually cooked, rather than eaten raw. Its stronger flavor makes it perfect for soups because it can stand up to a little bit of dilution. In this recipe we pair it with celery root to create a soup that is smooth, earthy, and slightly sweet. It's a nice match for succulent crab and the rich, nutty flavor of peanuts.

SERVES 8

CHINESE CELERY SOUP
WITH CRAB SALAD

MAKE THE SOUP: Separate the leaves from the stalks of the celery, setting aside the leaves from 2 stalks for the crab salad. Cut the stalks into 4-inch (10 cm) segments and put them in a pressure cooker. Reserving the peels, peel the celery root. Add the peels to the pressure cooker along with the water and salt. Cook at high pressure for 10 minutes. Let the pressure dissipate naturally.

Meanwhile, cut the peeled celery root into thin slices, put them in a bowl, and cover with water. Strain the celery stock and discard the solids. Put the stock and the sliced celery root into a clean pressure cooker. Cook for 7 minutes at high pressure. Let the pressure dissipate naturally. Open the top and add the celery leaves, stirring with a silicone spatula to incorporate them. Transfer the entire mixture to a metal bowl set in an ice water bath and let the mixture cool, stirring constantly and replenishing the ice as needed, for about 15 minutes. When the soup is cold, stir in the fish sauce.

SOUP

1 pound / 455 grams **Chinese celery** (about 1 bunch)

2 large **celery root** (about ⅔ pounds / 1,200 grams)

2 quarts plus ¾ cup / 2,000 grams **water**

1¾ teaspoons / 10.5 grams **fine sea salt**

1 tablespoon / 14 grams **fish sauce**

Put one-quarter of the soup into a blender and turn it on low speed. Increase the speed to medium-high and puree until smooth. Strain the soup through a fine-mesh sieve into a bowl. Repeat with the rest of the soup. Serve immediately or cover and refrigerate for up to 2 days. The color will slowly oxidize over time, turning it brown, so this soup is best served fresh.

MAKE THE SALAD: In a medium bowl, whisk together the peanut butter, crème fraîche, sake, salt, and Sriracha. Add the peanuts and celery leaves, and stir with a rubber spatula to blend. Pick through the crabmeat, removing any stray bits of shell or cartilage while keeping the pieces as large as possible. Add the crabmeat to the bowl and gently fold it into the sauce. Taste the salad and add a pinch of salt or a squeeze of fresh lime juice if desired.

TO SERVE: Divide the crab salad among 8 serving bowls. Put the soup in a large pitcher and pour it into the bowls, letting it pool around the crab salad. Serve immediately.

CRAB SALAD

4½ tablespoons / 75 grams **peanut butter**

⅔ cup / 150 grams **crème fraîche**, homemade (page 55) or store-bought

1 tablespoon / 14 grams **sake**

¼ teaspoon / 1.5 grams **fine sea salt**

½ teaspoon / 3 grams **Sriracha sauce**

1½ tablespoons / 15 grams **peanuts**, roasted (see page 39) and chopped

Leaves from 2 **Chinese celery** stalks, chopped

1 pound / 455 grams **lump crabmeat**

Fine sea salt

Fresh **lime juice** (optional)

TASTE & FLAVOR

Tasting is a complex experience. It may seem like a simple combination of what you smell and what you eat, but there is so much more to it than that. Simple flavors tend to fade quickly, leaving you mindlessly chewing your food without appreciating what you're eating. More complex flavor combinations encourage you to slow down and savor your food. Textural contrasts help capture your attention. They spark small changes in the dish so that each bite is unique. Tasting menus in restaurants—several small portions of different foods served in succession—are designed to combat palate fatigue while highlighting a chef's prowess, each small plate showcasing different preparations to keep diners excited by their meal. In truth, diners just need food that is well prepared and delicious with small accents of flavor to truly enjoy a meal.

There are five main tastes—sweet, salty, sour, bitter, and umami—accompanied by a wide variety of minor players like fat, heat, and spice. To make something exceptional, you need a little bit of each of these tastes. Think of them as puzzle pieces. The trick is figuring out how much to use and how to fit the pieces together. If one taste stands alone, you will quickly become bored with the dish. You need the play of tastes to create a nuanced dish. Salt can bring sweetness to the forefront without adding sugar; sweetness can downplay bitter; fat takes the edge off sour; umami increases the sense of richness; and bitter can soften saltiness.

Understanding how flavors work together helps create a better dish. The key is balancing the composition as a whole in order to avoid palate fatigue. We like to finish recipes with small touches—like the seasoned crème fraîche in the clam chowder (page 69)—that help pull everything into focus. The fresh herbs and lemon zest in the crème fraîche add a layer of aromatics that changes the palate's perception of the soup, making it seem brighter and fresher. The mixture melts unevenly, swirling around and adding creaminess and acidity to the chowder. Even more important, it guarantees that each bite will be slightly different so that you retain pleasure in the experience. All it takes is a small variation every once in a while to remind your brain to pay attention to what you're eating.

We all know how important the sense of smell is to experiencing flavor. What we don't often consider is the fact that there are two ways to smell: through your nose and through your mouth. One of the best examples we can think of is coffee. As children we smell its intoxicating aroma and want to taste it, but that first sip is usually a disappointment. To a child's palate, coffee is thin and bitter. Add some cream and lots of sugar and the child will be happy. That's because the mouth smell and taste experience of coffee is totally different from the nose smell.

What's interesting is the way that your brain can differentiate between the two types of smell. This means that while your perception can be influenced by the aromas surrounding your food, your perception of them will change once you hold them in your mouth. Wine tasting requires that you evaluate a glass of wine first by appearance, then by scent, and finally on the palate. Experienced wine tasters have no need to swallow because they know it is the act of "chewing" the wine in your mouth, allowing it to mix with air and wash repeatedly over your tongue, that will give you the full experience. While the aroma of a wine will tell you a lot about it, the flavor of a good wine is always a little different, richer, and more satisfying than the aroma alone. Even after you spit it out, a great wine will linger on your palate, providing a long finish that changes as it slowly disappears. When you sniff the wine again, your perception of the aroma will be affected by the taste of the wine. This is how our brains build a flavor vocabulary. That particular scent will now trigger the memory of that taste. We can teach ourselves to taste thoughtfully and discern flavors. All it takes is practice.

Texture is important because the ability to feel things with your tongue, as you taste them, is inherent to the pleasure of a meal. Somehow the action of touching your food with your tongue, feeling the way it moves inside your mouth, helps your brain figure out what it tastes like. As you hold food in your mouth, aromas are carried up into your nasal cavities and your perception of the scent of the food changes. Anyone who's ever had a shot of Novocain during dental work has probably experienced that food may smell the same but it does not taste as good until the anesthetic wears off. Even if you eat something that you've had a dozen times before, the flavors will be muted, as will be your pleasure in the experience because you will be unable to interpret the flavor the way you normally would. The tongue is an incredibly sensitive organ and while people tend to harp on the nose as the harbinger of flavor, it never works alone. That's why the best foods contain a variety of textures within one preparation. Think of fried chicken. It is that combination of crisp or crunchy crust, chewy skin, and tender, juicy meat all working together with the seasoning and the aroma and the mental associations to create food that people crave. Every bite is slightly different and it's messy and fun to eat. You have to focus on what you're doing, and your enjoyment increases because you are paying attention.

Every part of a dish contributes to how you experience it, and it would be a mistake to downplay the importance of any single factor. Still, once everything is on the table, it's time to stop analyzing, relax, and enjoy your meal.

WE HIT ON A BREAKTHROUGH TECHNIQUE IN THIS RECIPE:
freezer shucking. When you freeze and thaw clams, they open on their own, making it easy to shuck them with a spoon. This process also tenderizes the clams so they resist becoming chewy when you cook them. The shucking technique works with mussels and oysters as well, making it easier to use fresh shellfish at home. The biggest downfall to any chowder is usually the overcooked seafood, but here we add the clams at the last second before serving so that they are still tender and juicy when you take your first bite. Using the freezer shucking method, we've noticed that they stay tender when you reheat the soup, too. Finally, the seasoned crème fraîche adds a great flavor punch of fresh green herbs and citrus in the finished soup.

SERVES 8

NEW ENGLAND CLAM CHOWDER

Wash the clams thoroughly to remove any sand or grit. Lay them out on a baking sheet and put them in the freezer for at least 6 hours or until frozen solid.

Transfer the clams to a bowl and put them in the refrigerator to thaw. As they thaw they will pop open slightly; this will take at least 6 to 8 hours. Once all of the clams have opened, hold each one over a medium bowl to catch the liquid and use a spoon to scoop the meat out into the bowl with their liquid. Discard the shells. Store the clams and their juice in a covered container in the refrigerator.

Cut the salt pork into ¼-inch (6 mm) dice. Put it in the bottom of a large soup pot set over low heat and cook, stirring occasionally, until the fat has rendered and the pork is crisp, 8 to 10 minutes.

(recipe continues)

---

5 pounds / 2.25 kilograms **littleneck clams**

6 ounces / 170 grams **salt pork**

2 medium **leeks**

1 large **onion,** finely chopped

Fine sea salt

4 large **russet potatoes**

2 cups / 480 grams **crème fraîche,** homemade (page 55) or store-bought

1 cup / 260 grams **whole milk**

½ teaspoon / 2.5 grams **hot sauce,** such as Crystal

1 teaspoon / 5 grams **Madeira**

2 **scallions,** thinly sliced (15 grams)

Small handful of fresh **parsley leaves,** chopped

Celery leaves from 1 head, chopped

Grated zest of 1 **lemon**

Meanwhile, trim the root ends off the leeks. Thinly slice the leeks, removing the dark green outer layers as you move up the vegetable so that you are only slicing the tender white and pale green layers. Soak the leeks in a bowl of cold water to remove any grit. Spin them in a salad spinner to dry and finely chop. Once the salt pork is brown, add the leeks and onion to the pot, seasoning them lightly with salt, and continue to cook over low heat.

Peel the potatoes, rinse with cold water, and pat them dry. Cut them lengthwise into thirds and then cut them into thirds lengthwise again so that you end up with 9 long pieces, roughly resembling large French fries. Cut each piece at a 45-degree angle, turning the knife in the opposite direction each time to form rough triangles, about ½-inch (13 cm) across at the widest point.

Add the potatoes to the pot. Add 1 cup (225 grams) of the crème fraîche, the milk, and clam juices, reserving the clams for later. Bring the soup to a gentle boil and reduce the heat to maintain a bare simmer. Taste the broth and add salt if necessary. Simmer for 30 minutes. Add the clams and cook for 5 minutes until they are just tender and cooked through.

While the soup is cooking, put the remaining 1 cup (225 grams) crème fraîche in a medium bowl and whip to soft peaks. Add ⅛ teaspoon (0.75 gram) salt, the hot sauce, and Madeira and whisk well. Add the scallions, parsley, celery leaves, and lemon zest, and whisk well. The finished crème fraîche should have the texture of soft whipped cream. It can be stored in a lidded container in the refrigerator for up to 4 hours before serving.

To serve, ladle the soup into bowls and top each serving with a small dollop of the flavored crème fraîche.

CHOPPED HERBS AND ZEST FOR THE FLAVORED CRÈME FRAÎCHE

BAKED BEANS ARE ONE OF THOSE CLASSIC WINTER DISHES THAT people crave when the weather drops into the single digits. Using a pressure cooker means that you can satisfy your cravings at home on the very day that they strike. There is a generous amount of pork belly in these beans so they are a meal unto themselves, requiring only some crusty bread and perhaps a crunchy acidic salad to round things out. Leftovers are perfect for hot dogs or paired with a little mac and cheese for some cold-weather indulgence.

　　Adding a small piece of kombu to the pressure cooker when you cook beans does double duty: It makes the skins more permeable to ensure tender beans and adds flavor to the finished dish. The kombu can be fished out and discarded at the end of the cooking time and its flavor will have melted into the sauce, leaving behind only a deep savory quality. Kombu contains the enzymes needed to help break down the complex sugars that make beans hard to digest. This is good news for everyone at the table. We recommend using a 2-inch (5 cm) square piece of kombu for every cup of dried beans.

SERVES 8 AS A MAIN COURSE

NEW ENGLAND BAKED BEANS
WITH PORK BELLY

MARINATE THE PORK BELLY: Cut the pork belly into 8 roughly equal rectangular pieces. In a medium bowl, combine the salt, brown sugar, and pepper flakes. Put the pork belly pieces into the bowl and toss to coat the meat evenly. Transfer to a large plate, cover, and refrigerate for 2 hours. Discard any leftover salt mixture in the bowl.

PORK BELLY

3⅓ pounds / 1,500 grams fresh **pork belly**

5½ tablespoons / 100 grams **fine sea salt**

½ cup packed / 105 grams **light brown sugar**

½ teaspoon / 1 gram **crushed red pepper flakes**

BEANS

2½ cups / 500 grams **dried cannellini beans**

1 (4-inch / 10 cm) square piece of **kombu**

4½ cups / 1,000 grams **water**

5 teaspoons / 10 grams **garlic powder**

4 teaspoons / 25 grams **onion flakes**

½ teaspoon / 1 gram **crushed red pepper flakes**

2.6 ounces / 75 grams **candied ginger** (6½ tablespoons)

7 tablespoons / 150 grams **molasses**

1 (6-ounce / 170-gram) can **tomato paste**

1 cup / 225 grams **red wine**

1 (28-ounce / 794-gram) can **crushed tomatoes**

¼ cup plus 1 teaspoon / 70 grams **tamari soy sauce**

3 cups plus 2 tablespoons / 700 grams **water**

1 teaspoon / 3 grams **instant coffee**

COOK THE BEANS: Put the beans, kombu, and 4½ cups (1,000 grams) water in a pressure cooker and cook at low pressure for 5 minutes. Let the pressure dissipate naturally. Drain the beans, retaining the piece of kombu.

In a clean pressure cooker, combine the garlic powder, onion flakes, pepper flakes, candied ginger, molasses, tomato paste, red wine, crushed tomatoes, soy sauce, 3 cups plus 2 tablespoons (700 grams) water, and instant coffee. Stir the mixture together and add the beans, kombu, and pork belly. Cook at high pressure for 45 minutes.

Let the pressure dissipate naturally and serve immediately, discarding the kombu. Spoon the beans into 8 serving bowls and top each with a piece of pork belly. Alternatively, you can cool the beans and refrigerate overnight or for up to 3 days. Reheat in a covered pot in a preheated 250°F (120°C) oven for about 1 hour or in a pot set over low heat for 30 minutes, stirring occasionally.

MOLASSES is a by-product of the process of refining sugarcane to make sugar. Unripe or green sugarcane is often processed with sulphur to help extract the juice. Ripe sugarcane does not require the use of sulphur, and unsulphured molasses is considered a healthier choice. The sugarcane juice is boiled three times, each producing a different level of molasses, graded by both color and sweetness. The first boiling yields light molasses, the sweetest of the pure varieties. The second boiling yields medium or dark molasses and the final boiling yields blackstrap molasses, which is the least sweet version. It has a distinctly bitter edge and the highest level of nutrients. Treacle is the lightest and most refined variety of molasses on the market and is sometimes cut with cane syrup.

SEASONED
PORK BELLY

NEW ENGLAND
BAKED BEANS WITH
PORK BELLY ←

THIS SOUP BRINGS TOGETHER ALL OF OUR FAVORITE IDEAS about fall—apple picking and discovering new varieties in the orchard and at farmers' markets. A chill in the air and the gentle scent of wood smoke signal that it is the perfect time to start making soup for dinner. We use a blend of apples—usually Honey Crisp, Fujis, and Mutsus, if we can get our hands on them—which gives the soup sweetness and juiciness. Add some smoky bacon and sharp, tangy Cheddar cheese, and you've got an unbeatable combination. The crisp, gooey fritters take the place of croutons or bread and are fun to eat.

SERVES 8

APPLE-CHEDDAR SOUP
WITH BACON-CHEDDAR FRITTERS

MAKE THE SOUP: In a large saucepan, combine the onions, butter, and salt. Cook the onions over low heat until they are tender, 10 to 15 minutes. Add the apple juice and water, increase the heat to medium, and bring the mixture to a simmer. Add the cheese a handful at a time, whisking constantly to incorporate. Once the cheese has melted into the broth, adjust the heat to maintain a gentle simmer and cook for 30 minutes.

MEANWHILE, MAKE THE FRITTER BATTER: In a medium bowl, whisk together the flour, baking powder, and salt. In a separate bowl, whisk together the egg and milk, and pour the mixture over the dry ingredients. Stir with a rubber spatula until combined. Add the applesauce and stir to blend. Fold in the bacon, Cheddar, apple, and scallions, folding until thoroughly combined. Store in a covered container in the refrigerator until you are ready to fry, up to 1 hour.

(recipe continues)

SOUP

2 large **onions,** thinly sliced (about 1 pound / 500 grams)

4 tablespoons / 56 grams **unsalted butter**

½ teaspoon / 3 grams **fine sea salt**

1 quart / 900 grams **apple juice**

1¾ cups / 400 grams **water**

1 pound 2 ounces / 500 grams **sharp Cheddar cheese,** grated (about 4½ cups)

1½ pounds / 680 grams peeled, sliced **apples** (from 4 large or 5 medium)

Strain the soup into a clean pot, discarding the solids, and add the apples. Set the pot over medium heat, bring the soup to a simmer, and cook until the apples are tender and falling apart, about 30 minutes. Transfer the mixture to a blender and puree until smooth, 30 seconds to 1 minute, working in batches if necessary. Return the soup to the pot and keep warm while you finish the fritters, or chill the soup in an ice water bath and store it in a covered container in the refrigerator until you are ready to serve, or up to 3 days.

MAKE THE FRITTERS: Pour the peanut oil into a medium pot to a depth of 3 inches (8 cm). Heat the oil to 370°F (188°C). Add the batter to the oil by the tablespoonful and fry the fritters, turning occasionally, until they are deep golden brown and cooked through, 4 to 6 minutes. Transfer the fritters to a wire rack set over a baking sheet or a paper towel—lined plate.

In a medium bowl, whisk together the crème fraîche, scallion greens, and horseradish. Taste and add a few grains of salt if necessary.

To serve, divide the soup among 8 serving bowls and top each one with a dollop of horseradish crème fraîche. Arrange the fritters on a platter and serve alongside the apple soup.

FRITTERS

1 cup / 150 grams **all-purpose flour**

1 teaspoon / 6 grams **baking powder**

¼ teaspoon / 1.5 grams **fine sea salt**

1 large **egg,** lightly beaten

½ cup / 130 grams **whole milk**

½ cup / 125 grams **unsweetened applesauce**

3 slices **thick-cut bacon,** cooked and finely chopped

4 ounces / 113 grams **sharp Cheddar cheese,** cut into ½-inch / 13 mm cubes

½ cup / 55 grams peeled, diced **apple**

2 **scallions,** finely sliced

Peanut oil or canola oil, for frying

½ cup / 120 grams **crème fraîche,** homemade (page 55) or store-bought

2 **scallion greens,** thinly sliced

½ teaspoon / 2.5 grams **prepared horseradish**

THIS IS NOTHING LIKE THE SOUP THAT YOU CAN BUY IN CANS
and use as a base for casseroles. This is a soup that celebrates
the earthy flavor of the mushroom. The recipe calls for a blend
of mushrooms, but if you can't find them all at your local market
you can substitute different ones or up the quantity of oyster and
shiitake mushrooms. We add Indian lime pickle, readily available
in most gourmet or ethnic food markets, for its complex spicy
flavor. A generous splash of good Scotch adds depth and a hint
of smokiness, while the finishing touch of green sauce gives
the soup an herbal kick. If you make this for a smaller group,
you could use the leftovers in a mushroom Potato Gratin (page
121) by substituting the soup for the milk, and any leftover green
sauce will go equally well with meat or seafood.

SERVES 8

MUSHROOM SOUP

12 ounces / 340 grams
cremini mushrooms

12 ounces / 340 grams
shiitake mushrooms

8 ounces / 225 grams
portobello mushrooms

4 ounces / 115 grams **oyster
mushrooms**

4 ounces / 115 grams
maitake mushrooms

3 tablespoons / 45 grams
chopped Indian **lime pickle**

2 ounces / 60 grams
Ardmore or other smoky
Scotch

3 tablespoons plus
2 teaspoons / 60 grams
tamari soy sauce

3⅓ cups / 750 grams **water**

Green Sauce (page 136)

Remove the stems from all of the mushrooms and put the stems in a
pressure cooker with the lime pickle, Scotch, soy sauce, and water. Cook
for 5 minutes at high pressure. Let the pressure dissipate naturally.

Tear the mushroom caps into bite-size pieces and put them into a
large saucepan. Strain the mushroom stem stock over the mushrooms and
discard the stems. Set the pan over medium-high heat, bring the mixture
to a simmer, and turn the heat down to low. Cover the pot and cook for
5 minutes. Turn off the heat and let the mushrooms steep in the liquid
for 20 minutes. Turn the heat back on to medium and bring the soup to
a simmer.

To serve, divide the mushroom soup among 8 serving bowls and
put a spoonful of green sauce in the center of each.

WHEN WE TOOK ON CHILI, IT WAS A CHALLENGE. BRAISED BEEF often suffers from a dry texture, with all of the goodness going into the sauce. Great chili bridges the gap between flavorful meat and sauce so that both are happily eaten on their own. Together they become transcendent. This chili is made with a combination of ground beef and large cuts of meat on the bone. The resulting stew has a great texture. The chunks of meat make it more luxurious than a simple ground beef chili. The marrow from the beef shanks melts into the sauce, giving it richness and savoriness. You can serve the dish with the meat still on the bone, as we do, or you can take the time to remove the bones and gently pull apart the meat. Any leftovers can be shredded and served over pasta the next day for an equally delicious second meal. The light and crunchy cornbread waffles are the perfect partner.

SERVES 8

BEEF CHILI & WAFFLES

In a small bowl, whisk together the brown sugar, salt, onion powder, garlic powder, cumin, paprika, oregano, ancho powder, and jalapeño powder. Put the chuck shoulder, beef shanks, and ribs on a cutting board and season them all over with the spice mixture. Make sure to evenly and completely coat all of the meat with the spice mixture. Put the meat in baking dishes or on several large plates, cover, and refrigerate overnight.

The following day, cut the onions into slices that will fit into your meat grinder. Grind the onions and ají dulce peppers through the ¼-inch (6 mm) die and set aside.

Cut the chuck shoulder into strips that will fit through the grinder. Run through the grinder and reserve separately. (If you don't have a meat grinder you can pulse the meat in batches in your food processor until it is roughly chopped.)

Preheat the oven to 250°F (120°C).

Set a large saucepan over medium-high heat. When the pan is hot, add the rendered beef fat and heat until it shimmers. Put 2 beef shanks in

½ cup packed / 105 grams **light brown sugar**

2 tablespoons plus 2 teaspoons / 50 grams **fine sea salt**

5 teaspoons / 10 grams **onion powder**

1½ teaspoons / 3 grams **garlic powder**

1 tablespoon / 6 grams **ground cumin**

2½ teaspoons / 5 grams **smoked paprika**

2½ teaspoons / 5 grams **dried Mexican oregano**

2½ teaspoons / 5 grams **ancho chile powder**

2 teaspoons / 4 grams **jalapeño powder**

1 **boneless first-cut beef chuck roast** (about 2¼ pounds / 1.2 kilograms)

4 **bone-in beef shanks** (about 5¼ pounds / 2.4 kilograms total)

12 individual **bone-in beef short ribs** (about 6 pounds / 2.72 kilograms total)

3 medium **onions,** peeled

20 fresh **ají dulce peppers**

¼ cup / 56 grams **rendered beef fat** or olive oil

1 (6-ounce / 170-gram) can **tomato paste**

24 ounces / 675 grams **IPA beer** (2 bottles)

the pot and brown them on both sides, about 3 minutes per side. Remove the shanks to a large platter and then repeat with the other 2 shanks. Put 3 to 4 beef ribs into the pan, sear the top and the meaty sides, and transfer to a wire rack set over a baking sheet. Repeat with the remaining beef ribs. Add the ground chuck shoulder to the pan and use a wooden spatula to stir the meat, scraping up any caramelized bits stuck to the bottom of the pan. Cook, stirring, until the meat is lightly caramelized, about 10 minutes. Add the tomato paste and stir it into the meat. Add the ground onion and pepper mixture to the pan and stir to combine. Add the beer to the pan and cook for 5 minutes. Add the tomato puree, soy sauce, and water and let the mixture come to a simmer.

Arrange the beef shanks and ribs in 1 large or 2 medium roasting pans. Pour the hot sauce over the meat and cover the pans with foil. Bake until the shanks and ribs are fork-tender, about 6 hours.

Remove the pan or pans from the oven and let the chili rest for 30 minutes before serving. Leave the oven on to keep the cooked cornbread waffles warm. Or the chili can be cooled and kept in the refrigerator for up to 2 days before reheating and serving.

Scoop the chili into 8 bowls and serve with the cornbread waffles, Cheddar cheese, and sliced scallions on the side.

2 (24-ounce / 710-gram) jars **strained tomato puree**

9 tablespoons plus 1 teaspoon / 150 grams **tamari soy sauce**

⅔ cup / 150 grams **water**

Cornbread Waffles (recipe follows)

4.5 ounces / 125 grams freshly grated **Cheddar cheese** (1 generous cup)

1 bunch **scallions**, sliced

CORNBREAD WAFFLES

Corn flour is a great ingredient for baking, especially if you are not overly fond of the slightly crunchy texture of cornmeal in baked goods. It is closer in texture to durum than fine cornmeal. Bob's Red Mill makes a good one that can be found in many supermarkets. We like the flavor of cane syrup in these waffles, although in a pinch you can substitute molasses or maple syrup. The flavor will be different but still delicious.

1 cup / 150 grams **all-purpose flour**

1½ cups / 225 grams **corn flour** or fine cornmeal

2 teaspoons / 12 grams **baking powder**

½ teaspoon / 2.5 grams **baking soda**

1 teaspoon / 6 grams **fine sea salt**

2 tablespoons / 40 grams **cane syrup**

2½ cups / 600 grams **cultured buttermilk, homemade (page 54) or store bought**

1 cup / 260 grams **whole milk**

In a medium bowl, whisk together the flour, corn flour, baking powder, baking soda, and salt. Add the cane syrup, buttermilk, and milk and whisk until it comes together as a smooth, thin batter. Let rest for 15 minutes and it will thicken as the flours hydrate.

Preheat your waffle iron and make waffles according to the manufacturer's directions, being sure to make at least 1 waffle per person with a few extras. Waffles may be kept warm on a wire rack in a low oven until you are ready to serve.

4

SALADS

A RUSTIC SALAD, THIS RECIPE EMPHASIZES THE SWEET FLAVOR of the leeks. Instead of steaming them—as in the classic leeks vinaigrette—we grill them to soften their texture and add a slightly smoky flavor. Paired with a bright citrus vinaigrette and some fresh tarragon, they make a great warm salad that will go with almost any dish. We especially like the salad alongside a juicy Butter Burger (page 166) or with Slow-Cooked Hanger Steak (page 179).

SERVES 8 AS A SIDE DISH

GRILLED LEEKS VINAIGRETTE

8 medium **leeks**

6 tablespoons / 90 grams **fresh lemon juice**

1 teaspoon / 6 grams **fine sea salt**

1½ teaspoons / 6 grams **sugar**

4 tablespoons / 56 grams **lemon olive oil**

4 sprigs **tarragon,** leaves only, chopped

Rinse the leeks thoroughly in cold water. Remove any damaged exterior leaves and trim off any roots, leaving the core intact. Trim off the dark green leek ends and split the leeks in half lengthwise, cutting to, but not through, the cores, leaving the two halves attached. Soak the split leeks in cold water for 30 minutes, periodically swishing them around in the water to help rinse and remove any dirt from between the layers. Take the leeks out of the water and pat them dry. Inspect the leeks to make sure there is no dirt on them; if necessary, rinse and dry them again.

Put the leeks in a baking pan or baking dish just large enough to hold them. In a small bowl, stir together the lemon juice, salt, and sugar until the salt and sugar are dissolved. Add the citrus oil and stir to combine. Spoon some of the vinaigrette into the center of each leek, allowing it to seep between the layers. Spoon the rest of the vinaigrette over the leeks, cover, and refrigerate for at least 1 hour and up to 4 hours to let the flavors marry.

Preheat a grill to medium-high heat (400°F/205°C). Put a large sheet of heavy-duty foil on the countertop and top the foil with a piece of parchment paper. Put four whole leeks in the center of the parchment paper and fold the parchment over the leeks, crimping the edges to enclose them in the paper. Top the leek package with a second piece of foil. Line up the edges of the top and bottom pieces of foil and fold

(recipe continues)

them together, sealing the edges and creating another package around the wrapped leeks. Repeat the wrapping with the remaining leeks. Transfer any leftover vinaigrette from the pan to a small bowl, cover, and refrigerate. Put the leek packages onto the grill and close the lid. Cook the leeks for 20 to 25 minutes. The packages will swell with steam. To check the leeks, remove one package from the grill and carefully unwrap it. The leeks should be tender and lightly charred.

Remove the packages from the grill and let the leeks cool for 10 minutes. Open up each parcel and remove the leeks. Cut them into 1-inch (2.5 cm) slices and put them in a bowl. Add the chopped tarragon leaves to the leeks along with the reserved vinaigrette. Toss the leeks, taste for seasoning, and transfer to a serving bowl. Serve warm.

HERBS & SPICES

We love working with herbs and spices in the kitchen; dried spices add depth of flavor, while fresh herbs add brightness with a slight bitter undertone. Many spices are known to add a bit of stimulation as well. Peppercorns, chiles, ginger, cinnamon, alliums, mints, mustards, anise, and horseradish—these are all ingredients that prickle the tongue and wake up your senses. Herbs and spices add essential oils that can help slow down oxidation, aid digestion, and make your food taste better.

There are certain spices that we always have at hand. For baking we like cinnamon sticks and ground cinnamon, nutmeg, ground cloves, ground ginger, ground cardamom, and vanilla beans. Boyajian makes some wonderful citrus oils that have intense flavor, and we have tiny bottles of lemon, orange, and lime oils in our refrigerator. We are big fans of using Aftelier essential oils (available from Williams-Sonoma) in both sweet and savory recipes for the intense flavors that they can add in small doses. We love granulated garlic and onion powder. They are not a substitute for fresh; rather we often use the fresh and dried together in a dish to intensify their flavor. Other spices we like to have on hand are a variety of peppercorns, single varietal chile powders, sweet and smoked paprika, crushed red pepper flakes, ground cumin, fennel seeds, caraway seeds, star anise, and mustard powder. Beyond that our spice cabinet ebbs and swells according to what we are craving and cooking at any given time.

It's rare for us to use a single spice in a recipe, preferring instead to build a combination of flavors that work together to support a dish. You don't necessarily have to have a large number of flavors to make an impact, although there are many cases where spice blends involving many ingredients, like curry, are the backbone of a dish. Two or three supporting flavors are usually enough to make the primary ingredients sing. Think of building cocktails and how a dash of bitters can make the difference between something ordinary and something truly worth savoring.

When stuck for inspiration, we will open up a bunch of spices and smell them while thinking about the dish we're working on. It's an odd habit that always seems to work. The aromas are a guiding hand for what flavors will go well in the dish. Some ingredients trigger an immediate positive or negative reaction while others need to be sniffed a few times, perhaps in combination with spices we've already chosen before we decide.

There are some wonderful spice blends out there that have done the work for you. You'll see some of them in various recipes throughout the book. Most of them can be found in good supermarkets or gourmet stores like Williams-Sonoma, and occasionally even in a HomeGoods store for a fraction of their original cost. If you don't cook often enough to warrant a full spice cabinet, since spices do not last forever, a few good blends are a great addition to your pantry. We like to have a version of the North African ras el hanout on hand because its blend of sweet and savory spices and seasonings works well in a wide range of dishes, giving them a slightly exotic edge that we enjoy. One great curry powder, usually Japanese, is always in our cabinet because we just don't use enough to keep all of the ingredients on hand to make our own curry blends. And of course, no pantry is complete without Old Bay, that classic American seafood seasoning that is equally at home on blue crabs or potato chips.

THE KEY TO REVITALIZING THIS FAVORITE SUMMERTIME STAPLE
is a unique seasoning. Tomatoes and nori are both rich in
naturally occurring glutamates, which boost the umami qualities
in food. Bringing them together in this salad gives it a savory
flavor that lingers on your palate. This particular combination
of earth and sea is surprisingly harmonious; once you've tasted
it you'll swear that tomatoes and seaweed were meant to go
together. We like to use small tomatoes in this salad because
they have a great flesh-to-seed ratio and a nice texture, but
you can easily substitute your favorite sliced tomatoes instead.
Shichimi togarashi, often labeled simply togarashi, is a widely
available Japanese chile pepper blend that may contain up to
seven different ingredients, including sesame seeds, citrus zest,
and dried nori to balance and enhance the flavor of the chiles.

SERVES 6 AS A SIDE DISH

18 **small tomatoes** (not
cherry), each about 2 inches
/ 5 cm in diameter

1 teaspoon / 6 grams **fine
sea salt**

½ teaspoon / 1 gram
togarashi

6 sheets of **nori**

36 fresh **basil leaves**

2 **limes**

1 medium **jalapeño**

2 tablespoons / 28 grams
lemon olive oil

TOMATO & NORI SALAD

Fill a large bowl with ice water. Set a large pot of water over high heat and
bring to a boil. Use a slotted spoon or spider to lower 3 to 4 tomatoes at
a time into the boiling water to blanch for 15 seconds and then transfer
them to the ice water bath. Let the tomatoes cool for 5 minutes. Remove
the tomatoes and pat dry. Use a paring knife to peel off the tomato skins.
Reserve the tomato skins and put the tomatoes in a shallow baking dish.
Season the tomatoes with the salt and togarashi and cover with plastic
wrap. Set aside at room temperature for 1 hour. The tomatoes will exude
some of their juices.

Transfer the tomato juices to a blender and add the tomato skins.
Tear up 3 sheets of the nori, add them to the blender, and add 24 of the
basil leaves. Grate the zest from the limes onto a plate and leave the zest
at room temperature to air-dry. Juice the limes and strain the juice into
the blender. Turn the blender on low, increase the speed to high, and
puree until smooth. Transfer the nori vinaigrette to a bowl, cover, and
reserve in the refrigerator for up to 3 days.

Use a vegetable peeler to peel the jalapeño. Use a mandoline to slice it into slices that are ⅛ inch (3 mm) thick and put them in a bowl of ice water for at least 1 hour. This will help tame the heat of the raw peppers and give them a crisp texture.

Drain the jalapeño slices and pat them dry. Put them into a bowl, add the lemon olive oil, and mix to coat evenly. Spoon the nori vinaigrette onto the bottom of a platter. Arrange the tomatoes on the platter and then top the tomatoes with the slices of jalapeño. Drizzle the lemon olive oil from the bowl over the tomatoes. Sprinkle the dried lime zest over the tomatoes. Tear the remaining nori sheets and basil leaves into 1-inch (2.5 cm) pieces and scatter them over the tomatoes and the platter. Serve immediately.

THERE WAS A TIME WHEN EVERYONE WAS BUYING SMALL
butane torches to make crème brûlée at home. The problem
was that no one knew what else to use the torches for. We
discovered that they are very handy for charring fruits and
vegetables without actually cooking them. This gives them a
great caramelized outer layer while preserving most of their
texture and some of their fresh uncooked flavor; the char is
especially nice in salads such as this one, which is good in
summer and winter. This recipe makes a lighter and more
refreshing potato salad than classic mayo-based ones—and
there's no fear of letting this sit out on a picnic table. The heat
of kimchi is surprisingly addictive juxtaposed with the creamy
texture of the spuds. You'll end up with extra cucumber kimchi,
which is good, as it's wonderful on sandwiches and hot dogs. If
you happen to have some fresh herbs kicking around, they make
an excellent finishing touch to the salad.

SERVES 8 AS A SIDE DISH

CUCUMBER KIMCHI & POTATO SALAD

MAKE THE CUCUMBER KIMCHI: Slice the cucumbers into ¼-inch (6 mm)
rounds and put them in a bowl. Sprinkle the sugar and salt over them and
toss to combine. Put the cucumbers into a colander set over another bowl
to drain for 20 minutes.

Meanwhile, put the scallions, ginger, jalapeños, garlic, and lime on
a wire rack set over a baking pan and use a butane torch to lightly char
the surface of the vegetables and fruit on all sides. Zest and juice the lime
into a blender and add the ginger, garlic, whey, maple syrup, fish sauce,
soy sauce, and chile flakes. Turn the blender on low and increase the
speed to high to puree the pickling liquid into a smooth paste.

CUCUMBER KIMCHI

12 **baby cucumbers**

2 tablespoons / 25 grams **sugar**

2 teaspoons / 12 grams **fine sea salt**

1 bunch **scallions**, trimmed

About 7 inches / 50 grams **fresh ginger**

2 **jalapeños**, peeled

5 **garlic** cloves, peeled

1 **lime**

¼ cup / 55 grams **whey** or rice vinegar

3 tablespoons plus 1 teaspoon / 50 grams **Grade B maple syrup**

2 tablespoons / 28 grams **fish sauce**

1½ tablespoons / 25 grams **tamari soy sauce**

1 teaspoon / 2 grams **Korean red chile flakes**

POTATO SALAD

10 medium **Yukon Gold potatoes** (3¼ pounds / 1,480 grams)

1 tablespoon / 18 grams **fine sea salt**

Drain the cucumbers and put them in a medium bowl. Strain the pickling liquid through a fine-mesh sieve over the cucumbers. Thinly slice the charred jalapeños and add them to the bowl. Roughly chop the charred scallions, add them to the bowl, and mix everything together. Transfer to a covered container and refrigerate for at least 1 hour. The cucumbers can be stored for up to 1 week.

MAKE THE POTATO SALAD: Peel the potatoes and cut them lengthwise into quarters. Cut each piece of potato crosswise at an angle into irregular ¾-inch (2 cm) triangular pieces. Put the sliced potatoes into a medium saucepan and cover with water. Season the water with the salt and bring the potatoes to a simmer over medium-high heat. Turn the heat down to medium and cook the potatoes until just tender when pierced with a cake tester, 8 to 10 minutes. Drain and transfer to a large bowl.

Add half of the cucumber kimchi and stir to combine. Serve the potato salad immediately or cover and keep in the refrigerator for up to 5 days.

WE LOVE COLESLAW, BUT WE GET TIRED OF THE SAME OLD cabbage. So, we turned to kale, which is full of sweetness and holds its shape nicely whether it is braised or sautéed. Kale slaw has a great vegetal flavor that is softer and richer than cabbage slaw. We've put together a Russian dressing that adds raw vegetables and pickle juice to the mix. If you have any left over, try it on corned beef and pastrami sandwiches, with or without melted Swiss cheese. We also enjoy it with Oven-Fried Lemon Chicken (page 158) or Korean-Style Chicken Wings (page 156). This particular slaw holds up quite well for a few days in the refrigerator, which means that you get to enjoy every bite until it's all gone.

SERVES 8 AS A SIDE DISH

KALE SLAW
WITH RUSSIAN DRESSING

Remove and discard the kale stems. Finely slice the leaves about ¼ inch (6 mm) thick, then wash and dry them in a salad spinner. Put the kale in a bowl and add the grated carrot.

In a separate bowl, whisk together the mayonnaise, ketchup, pickle juice, chopped onion, chopped celery, chopped carrot, and horseradish. Pour the salad dressing over the sliced kale and carrots and stir to evenly coat the mixture. Put the kale slaw into the refrigerator to marinate for at least 2 hours and up to 24.

To serve, put the kale slaw in a bowl and crumble the Gorgonzola cheese over the top.

2 bunches **kale,** preferably Tuscan

1 large **carrot,** grated

RUSSIAN DRESSING

½ cup / 100 grams **mayonnaise,** preferably Duke's or Hellmann's

¼ cup / 65 grams **ketchup**

¼ cup / 60 grams **sweet pickle juice**

1 tablespoon / 15 grams chopped **onion**

1 tablespoon / 15 grams chopped **celery**

1 tablespoon / 15 grams chopped **carrot**

1 teaspoon / 5 grams **prepared horseradish**

4.5 ounces / 125 grams **Gorgonzola dolce cheese,** crumbled

KAMUT IS A HIGH-PROTEIN GRAIN RELATED TO WHEAT.

However, many people with wheat sensitivity are able to eat Kamut, perhaps because it has a lower gluten content. We like it because it tastes good, especially when you toast it and it develops a rich nutty flavor. This is a spin on classic tabbouleh salad. The lighter flavor and the slightly chewy texture of Kamut make it a nice change from the traditional bulgur wheat, and a pressure cooker makes cooking it a breeze. Coconut helps accent the natural sweetness of the grain and adds a hint of richness to the dish. We make this year-round and find it especially refreshing in the wintertime when salad greens are in short supply. You can find preserved lemons online and at gourmet groceries and spice stores; or you can try the recipe in our first book, *Ideas in Food*. Our local markets always have fresh parsley, and its refreshing herbal flavor can brighten up even the coldest afternoon.

SERVES 8 AS A SIDE DISH

KAMUT TABBOULEH SALAD

Set a large cast-iron skillet over high heat. When the skillet is smoking, add the Kamut to the pan. Let it sit undisturbed for 30 seconds and then begin to stir the Kamut with a wooden spoon. Cook until it begins to sizzle and crack, about 5 minutes. Remove the skillet from the heat and transfer the Kamut to a pressure cooker. Add the coconut water and ½ teaspoon (3 grams) salt and cook for 10 minutes at high pressure. Let the pressure dissipate naturally.

Strain the coconut water into a medium saucepan, reserving the cooked Kamut in a heatproof bowl. Set the pan over medium heat, bring the coconut water to a simmer, and simmer to reduce it to thick syrup, about 20 minutes. Pour the syrup over the cooked Kamut and stir to coat. Cool the Kamut and reserve in the refrigerator.

Preheat the oven to 350°F (175°C). Line a baking sheet with parchment paper.

1⅔ cups / 300 grams **Kamut**

4⅓ cups / 980 grams **coconut water**

½ teaspoon / 3 grams **fine sea salt**

1½ cups / 75 grams **unsweetened large coconut flakes**

½ teaspoon / 3 grams **sugar**

⅛ teaspoon / 0.15 gram **ground cinnamon**

⅛ teaspoon / 0.3 gram **ground cumin**

⅛ teaspoon / 0.4 gram **garlic powder**

⅛ teaspoon / 0.75 gram **fine sea salt**

1 bunch **parsley,** leaves only, chopped

3.9 ounces / 110 grams **preserved lemons,** finely chopped (about 5 tablespoons)

In a medium bowl, stir together the coconut flakes, sugar, cinnamon, cumin, garlic powder, and ⅛ teaspoon (0.75 gram) salt. Transfer to the baking sheet and bake until the flakes are golden brown, 4 to 5 minutes. Remove the baking sheet from the oven, stir the coconut, and let cool completely. Store the toasted flakes in a zip-top bag until ready to use, or for up to a week.

Add the parsley and preserved lemons to the Kamut. Stir and refrigerate for 30 minutes and up to 4 hours to let the flavors develop.

To serve, spoon the Kamut onto a large serving platter and sprinkle the toasted coconut over the top.

THE SIRLOIN CAP STEAK IS A TRIANGULAR PIECE OF MEAT THAT lies right above the top sirloin. It is an increasingly popular cut because it is relatively tender, flavorful, and economical. We employ a Japanese technique of crosshatching the steak to help keep the muscle fibers from contracting and toughening up the meat during the cooking process while still leaving it as one large piece for searing. Flipping the meat regularly as you sear it promotes rapid, even cooking of the meat. A salad of grapefruit, papaya, and watercress creates a sweet, peppery side for the beef.

SERVES 4 AS A LIGHT MAIN COURSE

THAI BEEF SALAD

PREPARE THE BEEF: Put the beef on a cutting board and remove any silver skin or large pieces of external fat. Cut a crosshatch grid into the top of the meat, cutting about ½ inch (13 mm) deep and leaving about ½ inch (13 mm) between the lines. Flip the meat over and repeat on the bottom, being careful not to cut all the way through the meat.

In a small bowl, combine the garlic, jalapeño, pickled ginger, sweet vermouth, soy sauce, and fish sauce. Put the meat into a gallon-size zip-top bag and add the marinade. Squeeze out the excess air and seal the bag. Turn the bag over a few times so that the meat is evenly coated. Refrigerate the meat in its bag on a baking dish or large plate for at least 24 hours and preferably 48, flipping the meat over twice a day, to allow the flavors to be absorbed.

MAKE THE SALAD: The day you are planning to cook the meat, grate the zest from the grapefruits. Transfer the zest to a small container, cover, and reserve in the refrigerator. Use a knife to cut the top and bottom off each grapefruit, exposing the inner segments. Stand the grapefruit up on a cutting board and pare off the skin, slicing it away from the top to the bottom, following the curve of the fruit. Once all of the pith has been removed, hold the grapefruit over a small bowl and use a paring knife to cut between the membranes and free the segments, letting them drop into the bowl. Squeeze the remaining membranes over the

(recipe continues)

BEEF

1 sirloin cap steak or **coulotte steak** (17.6 ounces / 500 grams)

1 garlic clove, thinly sliced

½ jalapeño, thinly sliced

0.35 ounce / 10 grams **pickled ginger**

2 tablespoons / 30 grams **sweet vermouth**

2 tablespoons / 33 grams **tamari soy sauce**

1 tablespoon / 14 grams **fish sauce**

¼ teaspoon / 1.5 grams **fine sea salt**

Rice bran oil or peanut oil, for frying

Leaves from 1 bunch **cilantro**

SALAD

2 grapefruits

5 teaspoons / 15 grams **palm sugar**, grated on a box grater, or packed dark brown sugar

1 tablespoon / 14 grams **rice vinegar**

2 teaspoons / 10 grams **fish sauce**

½ teaspoon / 3 grams **fine sea salt**

1 unripe **papaya**

1 bunch **watercress**, chopped into bite-size pieces

segments, catching the juice in the bowl. Remove the grapefruit segments from the bowl, cut them into thirds, transfer to another bowl, and set aside separately.

Add the palm sugar, rice vinegar, fish sauce, grapefruit zest, and salt to the bowl of grapefruit juice. Stir to dissolve the salt and sugar. Return the grapefruit segments to the bowl. Peel the papaya and cut it in half lengthwise, and remove the seeds. Use a mandoline to thinly slice the fruit. Add the papaya to the grapefruit vinaigrette and stir to blend with the grapefruit segments. Cover the salad and reserve at room temperature.

Heat a large cast-iron skillet over medium-high heat. Remove the beef from the marinade and remove any garlic or jalapeño slices that may be stuck to it. Season the meat with the salt. Add ¼ inch (6 mm) of oil to the bottom of the hot pan and when the oil shimmers, slide the meat into the pan. Turn the heat down to medium. Cook the meat for 30 seconds and gently flip it. Cook for 30 seconds on the second side and flip the meat again. Repeat this process until the meat has cooked for a total of 6 minutes.

While the meat is cooking, put half of the cilantro leaves on a platter large enough to hold the meat. When the meat has finished cooking, transfer it from the pan onto the bed of cilantro leaves. Cover the top of the meat with the remaining cilantro leaves and then invert a large platter over the meat to hold in heat while it rests. Let the meat rest for at least 5 minutes; the heat will release the oils in the herbs and they will permeate the meat while it rests.

Remove the top plate and transfer the meat, still covered in cilantro leaves, to a cutting board. Carve the meat into slices, cutting against the grain. Put the meat on a serving platter and add any juices and leftover cilantro from the cutting board or the resting plate. Add the watercress to the marinated fruit salad and mix gently to combine. Taste and add a pinch of salt if needed. Arrange the salad over the meat and serve immediately.

SEARED BEEF
RESTING IN A BED
OF CILANTRO

VEGETABLES & POTATOES

CREAMED CORN IS ONE OF THE BEST DISHES YOU CAN MAKE
with fresh corn. Use the large holes of a four-sided box grater to
cut the kernels from the cob; this leaves you with a great mixture
of cut kernels, scrapings, and juice. Stirring these up in a pot with
butter and seasonings activates the natural starches in the corn,
and you end up with a creamy bowl of sweet corn goodness.

We finish things off with an herb salad pesto. All that means
is we go through our garden and pick a few leaves of whatever
we have (usually somewhere between 8 and 12 different herbs)
and then blend them together in a pesto. Each time, it's a little
different and somehow all of the herbs come together into a
cohesive blend that is unfailingly delicious. Stir in the pesto at
the last minute to add depth and aroma to the flavor of the fresh
creamed corn.

SERVES 8 AS A SIDE DISH

SWEET CORN & HERB SALAD PESTO

MAKE THE PESTO: Put the herbs, cashews, garlic, and salt in a food
processor and pulse a few times to blend. Turn the machine on and
slowly drizzle in the olive oil. Turn the machine off and scrape down the
sides. Add the cheese and pulse to blend. Set aside.

MAKE THE CORN: Set a large box grater on a baking sheet and grate
the corncobs to remove the kernels and milk from the corn. In a medium
saucepan, combine the scraped corn, salt, and cayenne. Bring the mixture
to a simmer over medium heat and cook, stirring, until the mixture
thickens, 3 to 5 minutes. Turn the heat down to low and stir in the butter.

Spoon the creamed corn into 8 serving bowls and put a dollop of
pesto in the center of each portion. Serve immediately. Extra pesto may
be stored in an airtight container in the refrigerator for up to 3 days, or
frozen until needed.

HERB SALAD PESTO

3 cups / 45 grams assorted
fresh **herb leaves**

¼ cup / 28 grams **cashews,**
roasted (see page 39)

1 **garlic** clove

½ teaspoon / 3 grams **fine
sea salt**

¾ cup / 170 grams
extra-virgin olive oil

½ cup / 50 grams freshly
grated **Parmigiano
Reggiano cheese**

CORN

8 ears **corn,** husked

¾ teaspoon / 4.5 grams **fine
sea salt**

⅛ teaspoon / 0.25 gram
cayenne pepper

2 tablespoons / 28 grams
unsalted butter

GRATING THE CORN

CULTURED WHEY—YES, THE BY-PRODUCT OF CHEESEMAKING AND cultured dairy products—is an excellent ingredient for making pickles. It is a natural source for lactobacilli, which start fermentation. By adding them to the pickling brine via the whey you jump-start the process by increasing the number of bacteria in your liquid, speeding things up, so you can reach the desired flavor level more quickly, before the texture of the vegetables has softened too much. This means you end up with crunchier pickles with fully developed flavors. A pH meter is a useful and relatively inexpensive piece of equipment, because it lets you know without a doubt if your pickles are ready by measuring their acidity level. The abundance of zucchini in the summertime makes them a perfect choice for pickling. You can add spices and seasonings to your taste, but try the basic version first. You may be surprised by how much flavor the zucchini provide all by themselves. These simple pickles go anywhere you would normally use a dill pickle.

1¾ cups / 400 grams **whey** (page 55)

2⅔ cups / 600 grams **water**

8⅓ teaspoons / 50 grams **fine sea salt**

6 small **zucchini** (each about 6 inches / 15 cm long)

MAKES ABOUT 2 QUARTS

ZUCCHINI PICKLES

In a bowl, combine the whey, water, and salt and stir until the salt is dissolved. Wash the zucchini and cut crosswise into ¼-inch (6 mm) rounds. Add the zucchini to the bowl of brine and stir well. Divide the zucchini and brine evenly between 2 sterilized quart Mason jars. Put in pickle weights or take pieces of plastic wrap, scrunch them up into flattened balls, and put one in each jar to make sure the zucchini stay submerged in the pickling liquid. Cover the top of each jar with two layers of cheesecloth and use a rubber band to secure the cheesecloth to the jar. Put the Mason jars in a cool dark place to ferment. The fermentation will begin to show in about 4 days, with small bubbles forming in the jars. Continue to ferment until the pH is below 4.0, another 4 to 5 days, depending on the temperature of your storage area. Once the pickles are done fermenting, discard the cheesecloth, cover the jars with their lids, and store them in the refrigerator for up to 4 weeks.

FERMENTATION

Fermentation is a process of transformation, and it is making a big comeback. It seems like everyone—at home and in restaurants—is making cheese and vinegar and brewing up a storm. Home fermentation is economical and delicious. It allows you to take advantage of seasonal abundance, adds nutritional value to many foods, and makes them more digestible. Most important, fermentation adds flavor and makes food and drinks more delicious.

Beginners are often intimidated by the idea of fermentation. They don't realize that the open bottle of wine slowly turning to vinegar on the counter and that jar of sauerkraut in the fridge are examples of fermentation already occurring in their kitchen. Coffee beans and cacao beans are fermented before they are roasted. Miso, soy sauce, and salumi are all slowly fermented products with complex and haunting flavors. Sparkling kombucha and tangy kefir are popping up next to sodas in beverage coolers. In fact, from single-barrel bourbon to sparkling wine, fermented beverages make for festive occasions all around the world.

Fermentation is, generally speaking, the process by which carbohydrates are broken down by microorganisms and enzymes. The easiest way to facilitate this is to create a hospitable environment for positive microorganisms and let them go to work. In culinary terms it's easier to think of it as a process by which the sugars in food are broken down into acids or alcohols. This is an oversimplification, but it helps open your mind to the possibilities in your kitchen.

Sourdough starter is a great illustration of how two ingredients can transform into something very different from their original form. It is made by stirring together flour and water and then leaving them out at room temperature for a couple of days to ferment. We like to start small with ½ cup (113 grams) water and 4 ounces (113 grams) all-purpose flour. Stir them together and leave out at room temperature until the mixture starts to bubble and ferment. Once this happens, discard half and add another ½ cup (113 grams) water and 4 ounces (113 grams) flour. Repeat this process for three to four days, until the starter becomes very active and has a clean sour smell. Healthy sourdough starter looks alive; it seems to breathe, forming bubbles and moving around in its container. Once this happens it's ready to go. For a gluten-free starter, we use a fifty-fifty blend, by weight, of sorghum flour (sometimes called "sweet sorghum flour") and whole ground flaxseed meal instead of all-purpose flour; the process is the same.

If you feed your starter daily you will always have some on hand for baking. You can easily increase the batch by adding larger quantities of flour and water the day before you need to use it. On the other hand, if you want to take a break from baking, you can put it in the refrigerator to slow things down and simply feed it every other day (or discard the starter and start fresh when you're ready to begin again).

SCoBY (Symbiotic Colony of Bacteria and Yeast)—such as Kombucha mushrooms, kefir grains, and vinegar mothers—are easily purchased online and are used to ferment natural vinegars, sparkling beverages, and yogurts. These are live cultures that can be used to create fermented products at home. You can also buy dried cultures for lactic fermentation and cheesemaking from various sources online. Your favorite store-bought yogurt or buttermilk can be used to culture a new batch at home, which then can be used ad infinitum. Cultured whey, a by-product of homemade cultured butter and cheesemaking, can be used to kick-start your next batch of pickles (page 105).

Pickling was originally developed as a method of preserving the harvest through the winter. Nowadays shorter fermentation times can be used to preserve the fresh flavor and texture of ingredients as long as you keep in mind that the finished pickles will not keep as long as fully fermented versions. Today's quick pickles can focus on taste. We find that just a little lactic fermentation produces something quite delicious.

Most pickles are made by putting fruits and vegetables in a flavored brine and letting them ferment at room temperature. The salt works to keep away the bad bacteria and microorganisms until the lactobacillus bacteria can get going. Anywhere from 3% to 5% salt as the base of your brine will work nicely. A little whey in the brine will help get things going even faster. Here's the trick for pickling: Your ingredients **must stay submerged** in the brine. People sell pickle weights for this purpose, but you can also use a small ceramic disk or a crumpled ball of plastic wrap wedged under the lid of your container. As long as you have at least a 3% salt solution and your pickles are not exposed to the air in any way, your fermentation should never go awry.

Once the lactic fermentation has taken hold, the acid and alcohol that they produce take up the defense. A healthy fermentation has clear liquids and a clean sour smell. Fermentations can go bad, and it's usually quite clear when that's happened. Mold appears on the surface of your ingredients or they get slimy or malodorous. Trust your instincts; if it looks or smells off—and this goes for any type of fermentation—then add it to the compost pile. While these cases are rare and are usually caused by improper storage or failing to completely cover your ingredients with brine, it does happen occasionally and the best thing to do is start over.

A little bit of carbonation is a natural by-product of the process and shouldn't cause alarm. The fermentation process slows down dramatically in the refrigerator but doesn't stop completely. If pickles are left to ferment a little too long, they sometimes become carbonated. Biting into a fizzy pickle is an odd sensation. If you don't like the effect, the easiest way to alleviate it is to slice or chop the vegetables and let them rest for a few hours before eating them. The CO_2 evaporates out and no one will ever know it was there in the first place.

THE HEART OF THE ARTICHOKE IS ONE OF THOSE SPECIAL
ingredients that people go gaga for. When cooked properly it is surprisingly tender and silky, with a delicate, earthy flavor that makes everything else taste sweeter. We think of the heart as the pot of gold at the end of the rainbow, only reached after eating your way through layers of leaves, scraping the tender flesh from the spiky exterior with the edges of your teeth. Many people shy away from cooking artichokes at home because they think they are a lot of work to prepare. This recipe makes them easy, and the smoky flavor of the grill adds a whole new dimension to their natural sweetness. Artichokes generally appear in the springtime and are available throughout the summer. You can tell if an artichoke is fresh if it feels heavy in your hand and the leaves squeak slightly when you squeeze them together.

We figured out a handy way to make a cooked mayonnaise in the microwave. It is a little more shelf-stable than uncooked mayonnaise, and you don't have to stress if you don't have super-fresh organic eggs on hand. Since artichokes are usually served with either mayonnaise or melted butter, it made sense to bring the two things together into one satisfying dish.

SERVES 8 AS A SIDE DISH OR STARTER

GRILLED ARTICHOKES
WITH BROWN BUTTER
MAYONNAISE

GRILL THE ARTICHOKES: Preheat a grill to medium-high heat (400°F/205°C).

Halve the artichokes lengthwise. Use a spoon, melon baller, or small ice cream scoop to remove and discard the choke. Put the artichoke halves in a large bowl with the olive oil and salt, and toss to coat evenly. Lay a piece of parchment down on a cutting board. Lay 2 artichoke halves, cut sides down, on the parchment. Tuck 2 cloves of garlic underneath

ARTICHOKES

4 large **artichokes**

2 tablespoons / 28 grams **olive oil**

1 teaspoon / 6 grams **fine sea salt**

16 **garlic** cloves, peeled

BROWN BUTTER MAYONNAISE

8 tablespoons / 113 grams **unsalted butter,** melted

½ cup / 113 grams **extra-virgin olive oil**

¼ cup / 56 grams **fresh lemon juice** (from 2 lemons)

2 large **eggs**

2 large **egg yolks**

½ teaspoon / 3 grams **fine sea salt**

1/16 teaspoon / 0.125 gram **cayenne pepper**

3 tablespoons / 16 grams **Toasted Milk Solids** (recipe follows)

2 **lemons,** quartered and seeded

Maldon sea salt

108

each artichoke half in the hollow where the choke used to be. Wrap the parchment around the artichokes and then put the package on a large sheet of foil. Wrap the foil securely around the parchment-wrapped artichoke. Repeat with the remaining artichokes. Put the artichoke packages on the grill, close the lid, and cook for 30 minutes. Remove the packages from the grill and let them rest for 5 minutes.

(recipe continues)

MAKE THE MAYONNAISE: In a small bowl, stir together the butter and extra-virgin olive oil; set aside. In a large microwave-safe bowl, whisk together the lemon juice, whole eggs, egg yolks, salt, and cayenne. Whisk in the butter—olive oil mixture until combined. Microwave on high for 1 minute. Remove the bowl from the microwave and whisk the mixture. It will have just started to thicken on the edges of the bowl but will quickly thin out as you whisk it. Microwave on high for 1 minute more. Remove the bowl from the microwave and whisk the mixture; it should be thick and smooth. Strain the mayonnaise through a fine-mesh sieve and whisk in the toasted milk solids. The warm mayonnaise may be used immediately (it's good hot or cold). Once cooled, the mayonnaise may be stored in a covered container in the refrigerator for up to 1 week.

To serve, cut the artichoke packages open and put an artichoke half on each plate, cut side up. Spoon the garlic pieces back into the cavity where the choke was. Squeeze a lemon quarter over each artichoke and sprinkle with Maldon sea salt. Serve the brown butter mayonnaise on the side for dipping.

TOASTED MILK SOLIDS

MAKES 1 CUP / 80 GRAMS

Think of brown butter: The key is the toasted milk solids that fall to the bottom of the pan. Just the right amount of cooking transforms them into something deeply nutty and aromatic. The trouble with cooking milk solids in butter is the fat. Our first step in isolating them was toasting the milk solids (commonly sold as nonfat dry milk or powder) in the oven. The results were good, if a bit uneven. Then we realized that the pressure cooker would make uniform results easy. We put the milk solids in a Mason jar set on a rack in the pressure cooker for 90 minutes and the results were beautiful. Even better, once you've seen what the pressure can do, you'll realize that it can caramelize other ingredients just as easily. We like to use it for grains, nut flours, roux, yogurt, and white chocolate, for example.

1 cup / 80 grams nonfat
milk powder

Put the milk powder into a pint-sized Mason jar. Loosely close the lid on the jar. Put it on a small rack set inside a pressure cooker with 2 inches of water in the bottom of the chamber. Cook for 1 hour at high pressure and then let the pressure dissipate naturally. Remove the jar from the pressure cooker and let it cool to room temperature. Tighten the band on the lid if necessary. Toasted milk solids will keep at room temperature for up to 1 month.

THIS IS A SPICY ANTIDOTE TO YOUR AVERAGE, OVERLY RICH, one-note creamed spinach. The technique of pureeing the onion and garlic with the aromatics helps disperse the flavors evenly through the greens. The finished spinach is still creamy but with a kick of heat and citrus from the Citrus Kosho. Feel free to add a little more heat if you have a fiery palate. Pair this with poached eggs at breakfast or with Chateaubriand (page 171) at dinner.

SERVES 6 AS A SIDE DISH

CREAMED SPINACH
WITH CITRUS KOSHO

Put the onion, garlic, and citrus kosho in a blender and puree until smooth.

In a large saucepan, melt the butter over medium heat. Add the onion puree and salt and cook, stirring, for 4 to 5 minutes until the mixture has thickened slightly and lost its sharp, raw flavor. Add the spinach a handful at a time, wilting each new addition before adding the next, seasoning the mixture very lightly with salt after every few additions. Add the crème fraîche and bring the mixture to a simmer. Taste for seasoning and serve immediately.

1 small **onion,** chopped

3 **garlic** cloves

1 tablespoon / 15 grams **Citrus Kosho** (recipe follows) or store-bought yuzu kosho

4 tablespoons / 56 grams **unsalted butter**

½ teaspoon / 3 grams **fine sea salt**

1½ pounds / 680 grams **baby spinach**

½ cup / 120 grams **crème fraîche,** homemade (page 55) or store-bought

CITRUS KOSHO

MAKES ABOUT 1 CUP / 240 GRAMS

Japanese yuzu kosho is made by fermenting the zest from yuzu fruit with chopped chiles, salt, and seasonings. You can buy it ready made, but the fresh version is something special. Yuzu is hard to come by around here, so we opt for a multicitrus blend. The Boyajian brand oils add an intense kick of the individual citrus flavors. A few drops of citrus essential oils will also do the trick nicely, but if you don't have any on hand, your kosho will still be quite delicious. The combination of chiles and citrus in this condiment transforms into something bright and spicy and utterly addictive.

12 **limes**	3 drops / 0.25 gram **Boyajian lemon oil** or lemon essential oil (optional)
2 **grapefruits**	
2 **oranges**	
18 **lemons**	3 drops / 0.25 gram **Boyajian lime oil** or lime essential oil (optional)
2 **serrano chiles**	
3 stalks **lemongrass**	3 drops / 0.25 gram **Boyajian orange oil** or orange essential oil (optional)
2 tablespoons / 36 grams **fine sea salt**	

Zest the limes, grapefruits, oranges, and lemons into a small bowl. Thinly slice the chiles. Remove the tough outer leaves of the lemongrass to expose the tender hearts. Slice the heart of the lemongrass. Put the citrus zest, chiles, lemongrass, and salt into a mortar. Use the pestle to pulverize the ingredients to a uniform paste.

Juice and strain 1 lime and 1 lemon and add them to the mortar and stir to combine. Add the lemon, lime, and orange oils, if using, to the mortar and stir to combine. Put the citrus kosho into a small jar and refrigerate for at least 2 days to let the flavors develop. Citrus kosho can be stored in an airtight container in the refrigerator for up to 1 month.

CLASSIC EGGPLANT CAPONATA IS A BEGUILINGLY SWEET, SOUR, spicy, and salty dish from Southern Italy. Here we've taken the idea and turned it into a bright winter salad using butternut squash, raisins, capers, and cilantro. You'll need a good juicer for this recipe, but it's worth the extra effort. This caponata is great cold. If you happen to have some left over, it sautés up beautifully in a large skillet with some olive oil.

SERVES 8 TO 10 AS A SIDE DISH

BUTTERNUT SQUASH CAPONATA

5¼ pounds / 2.4 kilograms **butternut squash** (2 large)

1¼ teaspoons / 7.5 grams **fine sea salt**

½ teaspoon / 1 gram **crushed red pepper flakes**

¼ teaspoon / 0.5 gram **ground mace**

1 cup / 170 grams **seedless golden raisins**

4½ tablespoons / 35 grams **capers**

4 tablespoons / 60 grams **rice vinegar**

¾ cup plus 2 tablespoons / 200 grams **white grape juice**

¾ cup / 170 grams **dry vermouth**

1 **cinnamon stick**

½ cup / 10 grams **cilantro leaves**

Peel the squash and cut each one in half crosswise where the bulb meets the neck. Scoop the seeds and pulp from inside the bottoms of the squash and put them in a medium saucepan; set aside. Cut the bottoms into pieces small enough to fit in your juicer and set aside.

Cut the top half of each squash in half lengthwise and then halve each piece crosswise, for a total of 8 pieces of squash. Use a mandoline with a julienne blade set over a large bowl to cut the squash into a thin julienne. Any odd pieces that are difficult to julienne can be added to the cut-up squash bulbs headed for the juicer. Add the salt, pepper flakes, mace, raisins, and capers to the bowl with the julienned squash and mix with a rubber spatula to combine.

Juice the remaining squash pieces (discard the pulp). Transfer the squash juice to the saucepan with the squash seeds and pulp. Add the rice vinegar, white grape juice, vermouth, and cinnamon stick to the pan. Set the pan over medium heat and bring the mixture to a simmer. Cook for 10 minutes and then strain it over the julienned squash. Stir the squash so it is evenly coated with the hot squash juice. Cover the bowl and refrigerate for at least 8 hours and up to 3 days, stirring occasionally.

Fold the cilantro into the caponata. Transfer the salad to a serving bowl and serve immediately.

IT'S FUNNY HOW MANY EGGPLANT DISHES SEEM DESIGNED TO hide the flavor of the vegetable. This dish is all about the eggplant, highlighting its meaty yet tender texture. We smoke it and use some of the eggplant to make a tomato sauce and stuff the rest with basil and fontina cheese. It's a luxurious vegetarian dish with intense flavor and an ooey gooey texture from the melted cheeses. Serve it with a salad or steamed green vegetables; good bread is absolutely necessary for mopping up the sauce.

SERVES 8 AS A MAIN COURSE

SMOKED EGGPLANT PARMIGIANA

SMOKE THE EGGPLANT: Turn on an electric smoker or set up a stovetop smoker (see page 120). Peel the eggplants and slice them into ½-inch-thick (13 mm) rounds. Season with the salt and put them into 2 or 3 shallow pans that fit in the smoker. Smoke the eggplant for 1 hour and then cool at room temperature for 30 minutes. Weigh out 10.5 ounces (300 grams) of the oddly shaped or smaller pieces (roughly 3½ cups) and reserve the prettier slices in a covered container in the refrigerator.

MAKE THE SAUCE: Cut the 10.5 ounces (300 grams) of eggplant pieces into strips that will fit into a meat grinder and put them in a medium bowl. Cut the carrots, celery, and onion into pieces that will fit into the grinder and add them to the bowl. Add the garlic and then grind everything together.

Set a large saucepan over medium-high heat. Add the olive oil, and when it begins to shimmer, add the ground vegetables. Stir the vegetables with a silicone spatula and add the salt. Reduce the heat to medium and slowly cook the vegetables, stirring occasionally and scraping the bottom of the pot so they do not stick, until they are lightly caramelized and almost dry, 20 to 30 minutes. Add the white wine and cook for

(recipe continues)

EGGPLANT

3¼ pounds / 1,500 grams **eggplant** (about 3 large)

1½ teaspoons / 9 grams **fine sea salt**

Generous 1 cup / 21 grams fresh **Thai basil leaves**

1 pound / 454 grams **fontina cheese,** grated (about 4 cups)

½ pound / 225 grams **aged provolone,** grated (about 2¼ cups)

SAUCE

3 medium **carrots**

3 medium **celery** ribs

1 medium **onion**

3 **garlic** cloves, peeled

⅓ cup / 70 grams **olive oil**

2¾ teaspoons / 16.5 grams **fine sea salt**

1 cup plus 2 tablespoons / 250 grams **dry white wine**

1 (14.5-ounce / 410-gram) can **fire-roasted whole tomatoes**

5 minutes. Pour the can of tomatoes into a bowl. Use your hands to crush the tomatoes and then add them and their juices to the pan. Bring the mixture to a simmer, then reduce the heat to low, and simmer the sauce for 20 minutes. Turn the heat off and cool the sauce down in an ice water bath.

Preheat the oven to 350°F (175°C).

Set a 10 × 12-inch (25 × 30 cm) rimmed baking sheet next to your cutting board. Spoon an even layer of the smoked eggplant sauce over the bottom of the pan. Take the reserved eggplant and butterfly each slice by making a horizontal incision through the center that does not go all the way through the slice so that you can open it up. Open each piece, put one basil leaf and a handful of grated fontina inside, and press it closed over the cheese. Arrange the stuffed eggplant slices in the pan and cover them with the remaining sauce. Sprinkle all of the provolone over the top of the eggplant and cover the pan with foil.

Bake for 1 hour 15 minutes. Remove the eggplant from the oven, remove the foil, and bake until golden brown, about 15 minutes. Remove the eggplant from the oven and let rest for 10 minutes before serving.

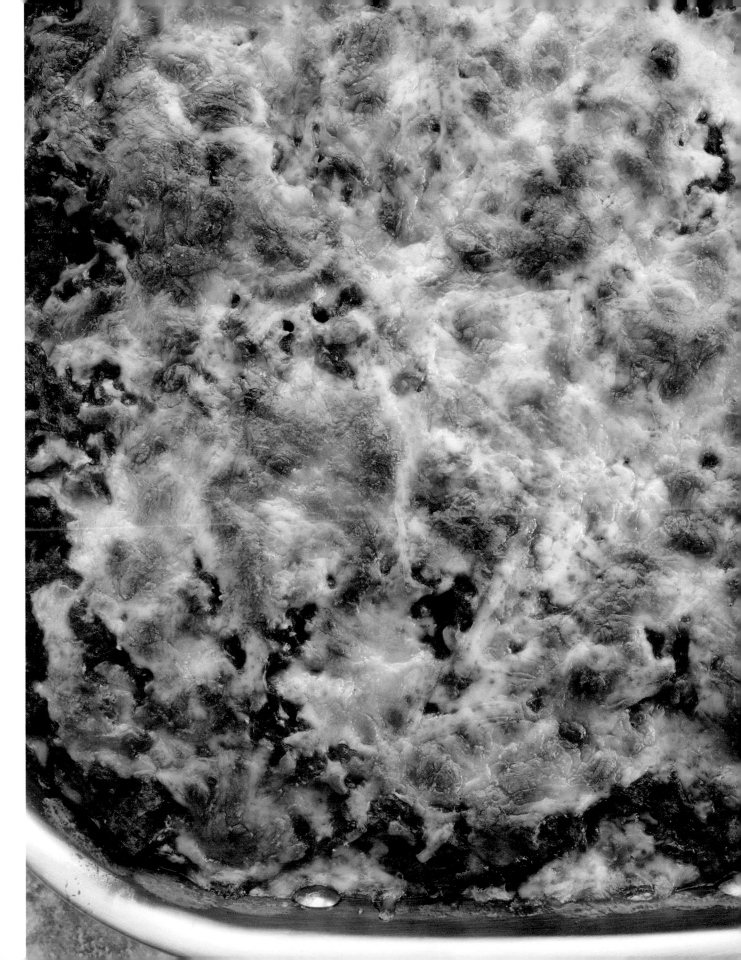

SMOKING

Smoke has a rich and layered flavor that, when added carefully, can enhance the inherent flavor of food. It multiplies the umami effect, naturally making smoked foods more savory and delicious. While smoking was originally used more as a preservative, today it is more about adding flavor. Smoking is clearly one of America's favorite pastimes. Though we love the flavor of smoke, rest assured that if it is not to your taste you can eliminate it from any of the recipes in this book. But we encourage you to try them as written because there are times when smoke can make everything taste just a little bit better, and that's what great cooking is all about.

Low smoldering flames create the best environment for smoking food. There are relatively inexpensive stovetop smokers readily available in most big-box stores and online. There's the Smoking Gun, a handheld device made by a company named PolyScience that allows you to inject smoke into a closed container like a covered pan or a zip-top bag and cold smoke just about anything. And let's not leave out the surprisingly wide variety of backyard smokers you can choose from, from manual to automatic, in sizes large and small.

If you're just starting out, you can rig your own stovetop smoker using a large roasting pan: Set a disposable aluminum pan in the bottom of the roasting pan and add a layer of wood chips or shavings. There is some debate about the wisdom of soaking your chips; truthfully, we don't bother with it. Set a stainless steel rack over them. Put food directly on the rack, or put it in a smaller, shallow pan and set that on the rack. Cover the roasting pan tightly with foil. Set it on a burner over medium-low heat and smoke for the desired time period. If you want to cold smoke ingredients, put them in a stainless steel pan set over a layer of ice and refresh the ice periodically as needed.

We have found that an outdoor grill is also the perfect tool for rigging an outdoor smoker, using disposable pie tins to hold wood chips or whatever else we may be using to generate the smoke. Put the wood chip material into the pie tin and put the tin directly on the grill grates. When it begins to smoke, put the ingredients to be smoked into a separate container in the grill and close the lid. Open the vents for some airflow and to help the wood chips smolder and smoke. If you're using a charcoal grill you can scatter a few wood chunks among the coals. For cold smoking, which flavors food without cooking it, set the grill on low and put the ingredients to be smoked in a container set over an ice water bath so they stay cool while in the grill. Generally speaking, cold smoking is best when it is done at temperatures ranging from 70° to 90°F (21° to 32°C). For long cold smokes, change the ice regularly and/or smoke for multiple shorter periods, refrigerating the ingredients between smokes to keep everything at optimum temperatures.

Once you've played with the technique, you can decide whether or not you want to invest in some of the smoking equipment mentioned above. Consider yourself forewarned, though: Smoking is addictive.

THERE'S A SPECIAL SYNERGY THAT OCCURS WHEN YOU COMBINE thinly sliced potatoes, onions, seasoned milk, and cheese and cook them long and slow. A potato gratin is so simple that you may wonder why we included a recipe for it. The proportions here are spot-on, so you can use it as a base technique with dozens of different variations. The 2½ cups of liquid can be dairy or stock or juice; in one of our favorite variations, we infuse milk with toasted onion solids to make an onion soup gratin. The same goes for the cheese: Gruyère is the classic, but you can use anything from Pepper Jack to Brie with delicious results. We like to serve this gratin as the main course of a meal, because the real problem with great potato dishes is that they are usually served on the side and we never get to eat as much of them as we would like.

SERVES 6 TO 8 AS A MAIN COURSE

POTATO GRATIN

2¾ cups / 720 grams **whole milk**

½ cup / 120 grams **crème fraîche,** homemade (page 55) or store-bought, or heavy cream

2 large **eggs**

¼ teaspoon / 0.5 gram freshly grated **nutmeg**

1 teaspoon / 6 grams **fine sea salt**

½ medium **onion**

4 large **russet potatoes,** peeled

10 ounces / 285 grams **Gruyère cheese,** freshly grated (about 2½ cups)

Preheat the oven to 350°F (175°C). Butter a 3-quart (2.8-liter) gratin dish.

In a large bowl, combine the milk and crème fraîche. Whisk in the eggs, nutmeg, and salt. Use a mandoline to thinly slice the onion and potatoes directly into the bowl of milk. Mix gently with your hands to blend and coat. Take half the onions and potatoes and spread them evenly in the bottom of the prepared gratin dish. Add half of the cheese in an even layer on top. Add the remaining onions and potatoes, making sure the top is smooth and even. Pour any remaining liquid into the dish, top with the remaining cheese, and cover with foil.

Bake for 1 hour. Remove the foil, rotate the gratin dish, and cook until the top is a deep golden brown, about 30 minutes. Serve hot.

IT SEEMS THAT EVERYONE CHASES THE PERFECT FRENCH FRY.
Our technique is to soak them in salted water and then steam them in the pressure cooker to hydrate the starches and gelatinize them before a final frying round. This produces perfectly cooked potatoes encased in a thin, crisp outer shell. A sprinkling of salt is all you really need to finish them off.

SERVES 4 AS A SIDE DISH

6⅔ cups / 1,500 grams **water**

2½ tablespoons / 45 grams **fine sea salt,** plus more for seasoning the fries

6 large **russet potatoes**

Rice bran oil or peanut oil, for frying

FRENCH FRIES

In a large bowl, combine the water and salt and stir until the salt is dissolved.

Peel the potatoes. Square off the top and bottom of each potato and then trim a small slice off the bottom of each one so that it lies flat on the cutting board. Cut the potato into ⅜-inch-thick (1 cm) planks. Lay each plank flat on the cutting board and cut lengthwise into ⅜-inch-wide (1 cm) batons. Put the potato batons in the bowl of salt water and let them soak for 2 to 3 hours.

Drain the potatoes and discard the water. Put the potatoes in a bowl that fits easily inside your pressure cooker. Put 2 inches (5 cm) of water in the cooker and set a small rack inside. Put the bowl on the rack and cook at high pressure for 5 minutes. Let the pressure dissipate naturally. Remove the lid of the pressure cooker and immediately remove the potatoes from the bowl and lay them out on a wire rack to cool to room temperature, about 30 minutes. (If you leave them to cool in the bowl they will stick to each other and to the bowl.) Refrigerate the potatoes, uncovered, for up to 6 hours, until you are ready to fry, or cover when completely cold and refrigerate for up to 24 hours.

Preheat the oven to 250°F (120°C).

Fill a large pot with 2 inches (5 cm) of oil and heat it to 400°F (205°C). Put about one-quarter of the potatoes in the oil and stir them with a metal spider skimmer. The temperature should drop to about 375°F (190°C). Cook the potatoes until they are a deep golden brown on the outside and cooked through, about 5 minutes. It's important to cook these potatoes all the way through or they will steam as they cool and lose their crisp texture. Transfer the fries to a wire rack and season generously with salt. Put the rack with the fries into the warm oven while frying the remaining batches. Serve hot.

WHEN WE ROAST OUR POTATOES, WE NESTLE THEM INTO A BED of onions and lemons. The flavors slowly penetrate the spuds, and the lemons and onions soften and caramelize into an almost marmalade-like texture. Toss in chopped rosemary at the very end and the heat from the baking pan is enough to release the natural oils and cause it to perfume the entire dish. Just a few ingredients, used to their best advantage.

SERVES 6 TO 8 AS A SIDE DISH

LEMON ROASTED POTATOES

2 pounds 3 ounces / 1,000 grams **new potatoes**

1 medium **yellow onion**

2 small **lemons,** preferably Meyer

1 teaspoon / 6 grams **fine sea salt**

1 teaspoon / 5 grams **olive oil**

⅔ cup / 150 grams **unsalted butter**

1 teaspoon / 1.5 grams chopped fresh **rosemary**

Preheat the oven to 425°F (225°C).

Set a stovetop steamer over medium heat. Add the potatoes. Adjust the heat to maintain a gentle simmer and steam the potatoes until tender when pierced with a cake tester, about 10 minutes.

Meanwhile, halve the onion through the root end so that there is a piece of core at the end of both halves holding the layers together. Cut off a small slice at one end of each lemon so that you just expose the inner fruit. Use a mandoline or sharp chef's knife to thinly slice the onion and lemons, discarding the uncut end of the lemon, any seeds, and onion cores when you are done. Mix them together with your hands in a medium bowl and season with the salt.

Once the potatoes are cooked, transfer them to a large plate to cool slightly and then use a paring knife to peel off the skins and discard. Cut each potato in half.

Put the olive oil in a heavy 9 × 13-inch (23 × 33 cm) roasting pan and rub it around the inside of the pan to coat it thoroughly. Layer the onions and lemons in the bottom of the dish. Lay the potatoes cut side down on top of them. Thinly slice the butter and lay one slice over each potato and scatter any extra over the top. Bake for 25 minutes. Rotate the dish and bake until the potatoes are a deep golden brown, about 10 more minutes.

Remove the dish from the oven and scatter the rosemary over the potatoes. Let the dish rest for 5 minutes before serving so that the herb can permeate the dish. Serve from the roasting pan so the potatoes will remain crisp.

THESE GNOCCHI ARE EASY TO PUT TOGETHER AND FOOLPROOF:
There is no fear of overmixing with choux paste as the base.
Make sure your potato flakes contain nothing but dehydrated
potatoes. You can mix the batter in advance and then cook the
gnocchi to order. If you are a fan of barbecue potato chips, you'll
love the surprise of smoky flavor in this pasta.

SERVES 8 AS A SIDE DISH

BARBECUE POTATO GNOCCHI

Preheat the oven to 350°F (175°C).

Spread the potato flakes on a baking sheet and toast in the oven
for 5 minutes, then stir. Continue toasting until they are a deep, golden
brown, about 5 minutes longer. Remove from the oven and let cool at room
temperature. Once cool, grind in a food processor to make a fine flour.

In a medium saucepan, combine the beer, barbecue sauce, butter,
garlic powder, onion powder, garam masala, salt, nutmeg, and pepper.
Bring to a simmer over medium heat. Add the ground potato flakes and
flour and stir until the dough forms a ball and pulls away from the edges,
about 1 minute. Cook, stirring, for 1 minute more until a light film forms
on the bottom of the pot. Transfer the dough to a stand mixer fitted
with the paddle attachment and add the cheese. Paddle the dough for
5 minutes to cool and then start adding the eggs one at a time, allowing
each to be incorporated into the dough. Turn the mixer off and let
the dough cool to room temperature, about 30 minutes. It can be used
immediately or you can chill it and shape it cold.

Set a large pot of salted water over high heat and bring to a boil.
Transfer the dough to a piping bag fitted with a ½-inch (13 mm) plain tip.
Working quickly, pipe the gnocchi over the boiling water, using a paring
knife to cut off ½-inch (13 mm) portions and letting them fall into the
water. Cook until just set and tender, 3 to 5 minutes. You can check by
cutting one open and tasting it. Drain lightly and transfer to a large bowl.

Melt the butter in a large pan over medium heat. Add the gnocchi
and sauté until golden brown, 2 minutes. Gently fold the Parmigiano into
the gnocchi. Serve hot.

2 cups / 120 grams **potato flakes**

7 ounces / 195 grams **IPA beer**

⅔ cup / 165 grams **barbecue sauce**

12½ tablespoons / 175 grams **unsalted butter**

1 tablespoon / 6 grams **garlic powder**

1 tablespoon / 6 grams **onion powder**

2½ teaspoons / 5 grams **garam masala**

1 teaspoon / 6 grams **fine sea salt**

½ teaspoon / 1 gram **freshly grated nutmeg**

½ teaspoon / 1 gram **cracked black pepper**

1 cup minus 1 tablespoon / 140 grams **all-purpose flour**

6 ounces / 165 grams **Cheddar cheese,** grated (about 1½ cups)

6 large **eggs**

4 tablespoons / 56 grams **unsalted butter,** sliced

1 ounce / 30 grams **Parmigiano Reggiano cheese,** freshly grated (about 5 tablespoons)

THIS IS A NEW SPIN ON THE CLASSIC FRENCH ALIGOT—AN
elastic potato puree with Cantal cheese. We opt for Japanese yams for their sweet, earthy flavor and a blend of three different cheeses. The finishing touch of fermented black bean powder adds depth and rounds out the flavor in an unusual way. Using the microwave to pull this dish together makes for a smoother finished dish that has less of a tendency to break and become greasy.

SERVES 8 AS A SIDE DISH

JAPANESE YAM & CHEESE

3 large **Japanese yams** (about 3 pounds / 1,325 grams total)

7 ounces / 200 grams **aged provolone cheese,** grated (about 1¾ cups)

6 ounces / 175 grams **aged Cheddar cheese,** grated (about 1½ cups)

¾ teaspoon / 4.5 grams **fine sea salt**

6.5 ounces / 185 grams **Brie cheese,** rind removed

1 tablespoon / 9 grams **fermented black bean powder** (optional)

Preheat the oven to 350°F (175°C). Line a baking sheet with parchment paper.

Poke the yams with a cake tester or skewer in several places. Put on the baking sheet and bake until completely tender, about 2 hours. Remove the pan from the oven and let the yams cool for 20 minutes at room temperature. Cut them in half lengthwise and scoop the warm flesh directly into a food processor, discarding the skins. Puree, occasionally stopping the machine to scrape down the sides, until smooth. At this point you can cool the puree down and refrigerate it until you are ready to finish the dish, or for up to 2 days.

In a bowl, stir together the provolone and Cheddar. Put the cold yam puree into a large microwave-safe bowl and microwave on high for 1 minute. Remove the bowl from the microwave. Add the salt and Brie and use a rubber spatula to stir the mixture. Microwave on high for 1 minute more. Remove the bowl from the microwave, add a handful of the grated cheese mixture, and stir to combine. Microwave on high for 1 minute more. Remove the bowl from the microwave and add another handful of the cheese mixture. Use a rubber spatula to beat the cheese into the yams and microwave on high for 1 minute more. Continue heating and adding cheese for a total cooking time of 10 minutes. The mixture should be hot and glossy with an elastic quality.

Transfer to a shallow serving dish and use a fine-mesh sieve to dust the fermented black bean powder over the top.

BEATING THE CHEESE INTO THE YAMS

SMOKED TROUT &
 SUNFLOWER
 SEED
 RISOTTO 132

PUMPERNICKEL
 FRIED FLUKE
 WITH THOUSAND
 ISLAND
 DRESSING 135

SEARED SCALLOPS
 WITH GREEN
 SAUCE 136

FISH TACOS 139

GINGER SCALLION
 SQUID 144

SMOKED MAPLE &
 MISO GLAZED
 WILD ALASKAN
 SALMON 146

COCONUT STEAMED
 HALIBUT 148

FISH & SHELLFISH

AS KIDS, WE THOUGHT IT WAS SO FUN TO EAT SUNFLOWER
seeds, sucking on the tiny shells and popping out the little
kernels. Now as adults, we've found that cooking them in
the pressure cooker makes them tender, another neat trick.
Pureeing some of the cooked seeds and folding them back in
with the whole ones creates a texture similar to a good risotto—
but one that can be made in advance and reheated, and is filled
with protein and fiber from the seeds. When we first came up
with this dish in 2005, people were delighted with the unusual
flavor and texture. We've refined it over the years and it's become
something of a signature. It's rich and luxurious with a sweet
nuttiness that goes beautifully with smoked trout.

SERVES 8 AS AN APPETIZER

SMOKED TROUT & SUNFLOWER SEED RISOTTO

4 tablespoons / 56 grams **unsalted butter**
2 tablespoons / 28 grams **extra-virgin olive oil**
1 small **white onion,** chopped
½ teaspoon / 3 grams **fine sea salt**
16 ounces / 455 grams **hulled sunflower seeds**
½ cup / 113 grams **dry vermouth**
3½ cups / 800 grams **chicken broth** or vegetable stock
¼ cup / 15 grams **julienned Kombu**
1 whole **smoked trout** (about 1 pound / 454 grams)
2 ounces / 57 grams **Piave Vecchio** or **Parmigiano Reggiano cheese,** grated (about 9 tablespoons)
Fine sea salt and **freshly ground black pepper**
Grated zest of 1 **lemon**
4 **scallions,** finely sliced
3 tablespoons / 45 grams **crème fraîche,** homemade (page 55) or store-bought

Melt 1 tablespoon (14 grams) of the butter in a pressure cooker and
add the olive oil. Add the onion and cook, stirring, until tender, 2 to
3 minutes. Season with ¼ teaspoon (1.5 grams) of the salt. Add the
sunflower seeds and continue to cook until the seeds are lightly toasted,
about 5 minutes. Add the vermouth. Continue to cook until the onions
are nearly dry and the seeds are lightly glazed, about 10 minutes.

Add the chicken broth, Kombu, and remaining ¼ teaspoon
(1.5 grams) salt and cover the pressure cooker. Cook at high pressure for
10 minutes. Let the pressure dissipate naturally. Strain the liquid from the
seeds, reserving the liquid separately, and return the seeds to the cooker.
Scoop out one-third of the seeds and puree in a blender with the cooking
liquid until smooth. Stir into the reserved sunflower seeds. The risotto
can be finished immediately or chilled and refrigerated in a covered
container for up to 48 hours.

Put the risotto in a medium saucepan and bring to a simmer over medium heat, stirring occasionally. If the texture seems a bit thick, add a little water to thin it out.

Meanwhile, remove the skin from the smoked trout and flake it into large pieces, discarding any bones.

When the risotto is hot, stir in the remaining 3 tablespoons (42 grams) butter and two-thirds of the cheese, and taste to check the seasoning, adding salt and pepper if desired. Fold in the lemon zest, sliced scallions, crème fraîche, and flaked trout and cook for 5 minutes to warm up the trout.

Spoon the risotto into 8 serving bowls and top with the remaining cheese and some freshly ground black pepper. Serve immediately.

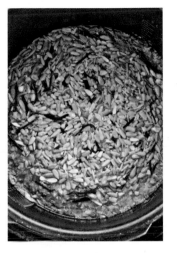

Audrey Saunders awakened us to the possibilities of **VERMOUTH** several years ago at an event where she served white vermouth infused with apples. It made for a complex and wonderful drink that seemed like so much more than the sum of its parts. It prompted us to take a closer look at the wine. Vermouth is a fortified wine that has been infused with a variety of botanicals. The name comes from wormwood, one of the original ingredients that was later outlawed for being poisonous. Vermouth comes in two varieties commonly associated with cocktails, dry and sweet. Dry vermouth, first made by Joseph Noilly of France, is made from white wine and is typically used for martinis. Sweet vermouth, first made commercially by Antonio Benedetto Carpano in Italy, has a red wine base and is commonly used in Manhattans. Noilly Pratt dry vermouth and a variety of sweet vermouths from Carpano, notably Punt e Mes, to this day are considered delicious examples of this wine. An open bottle of vermouth will keep well for up to six months in the refrigerator and adds great flavor to recipes, making it perfect for both the kitchen and the bar.

JUST-PRESSURE-COOKED
SUNFLOWER SEEDS; FINISHED
SUNFLOWER SEED RISOTTO

A PUMPERNICKEL BATTER IMPARTS ITS SPICY FLAVOR AS AN accent to fried fish. We use a whipped cream dispenser to lighten the beer batter even further so that it fries up like the most delicate tempura you've ever tasted. It shatters under your teeth, giving way to the firm juicy fish underneath. Paired with Thousand Island dressing, it makes a delicious twist on classic fried fish.

SERVES 4 TO 6

PUMPERNICKEL FRIED FLUKE
WITH THOUSAND ISLAND DRESSING

Put the caraway seeds in a small saucepan set over medium heat and cook until the caraway is fragrant, about 3 minutes. Remove the pan from the heat and transfer the seeds to a plate to cool. Grind the seeds in a spice grinder to a fine powder and then sift through a fine-mesh sieve into a bowl. Add the rye flour, all purpose flour, cornstarch, tapioca starch, cocoa powder, egg white powder, sugar, salt, and baking soda and stir to combine. Reserve until you're ready to fry the fish.

Preheat the oven to 250°F (120°C). Set a wire rack in a baking sheet. Stir the chopped pickles into the dressing.

Cut the fluke fillets in half through their middle seam and remove any random bones. Put some rye flour in a shallow baking dish. Pour 2 inches (5 cm) of peanut oil in the bottom of a large pot and heat to 350°F (177°C). Dredge each fillet in rye flour, shaking off the excess, and then put the fillets onto a baking sheet.

Add the beer and molasses to the flour mixture and stir to combine. Pour the batter into the canister of a whipped cream dispenser and charge with one CO_2 charge. Shake the canister vigorously. Extrude some of the batter into a large bowl. Dip 2 of the fluke fillets in the batter and then slowly lower them into the hot oil. Cook the fish for 2 minutes and then flip them over. Cook the fish for 2 minutes more. Transfer them to the rack in the baking sheet and put in the warm oven while frying the remaining fish. Serve immediately, topped with whole pickle slices, and with the dressing on the side.

1 tablespoon / 7 grams **caraway seeds**

10 tablespoons / 65 grams **dark rye flour,** plus more for dredging the fish

⅓ cup / 50 grams **all-purpose flour**

3½ tablespoons / 25 grams **cornstarch**

3 tablespoons / 18 grams **tapioca starch**

5½ teaspoons / 15 grams **Dutch-process cocoa powder**

1½ tablespoons / 6 grams **egg white powder**

1 teaspoon / 4 grams **sugar**

¼ teaspoon / 1.5 grams **fine sea salt**

⅛ teaspoon / 0.75 gram **baking soda**

1 cup / 150 grams chopped **Zucchini Pickles** (page 105), plus whole pickle slices for serving

Russian Dressing (page 95)

12 ounces / 338 grams **IPA beer**

2 teaspoons / 15 grams **molasses**

2 pounds / 1,000 grams **fluke fillets**

Peanut oil or canola oil, for frying

WE HAVE A FAVORITE TRICK FOR SEAFOOD: A QUICK 10-MINUTE
brine in a 0.5% salt solution. The amount of salt is calculated
as a percentage of the weight of the amount of water used for
the brine. This soaking period firms up the outer layer of the
flesh and rinses off exterior proteins so that the seafood cooks
up cleanly, with less undesirable white albumen forming on the
outside of the fish. The albumen is less of an issue with scallops,
but we do find that they sauté up more evenly and seem to
have a slightly firmer texture once cooked. When searing, it's
important to use a heavy pan and leave the scallops alone long
enough for them to form a beautiful crust. As a last step, the
scallops are basted with butter to highlight their sweet flavor.
The green sauce then mixes with the natural juices of the
scallops on the plate to take this dish into the stratosphere.

SERVES 8

SEARED SCALLOPS
WITH GREEN SAUCE

MAKE THE SAUCE: In a small saucepan, combine the garlic, olive oil, and
pepper flakes. Bring to a simmer over medium heat and turn the heat
down to low. Cook the garlic until it is just turning golden brown, about
5 minutes. Remove the pan from the heat. Put the herbs in a blender and
pour the hot oil and garlic over them. Turn the blender on low speed.
Increase the speed to medium-high and add the fish sauce. Continue
to blend until smooth. Turn the blender off and strain the green sauce
through a fine-mesh sieve. Set the sauce aside to cool.

PREPARE THE SCALLOPS: Remove the tough "catch" muscle from
the sides of the scallops. Put the water into a large bowl and stir in the
salt until it is dissolved. Put the scallops in the brine for 10 minutes.
Remove the scallops from the brine, pat dry, and continue to the next step
or refrigerate on a covered plate for up to 24 hours.

(recipe continues)

SAUCE

10 medium **garlic** cloves,
sliced

7 tablespoons / 100 grams
olive oil

¼ teaspoon / 0.5 gram
crushed red pepper flakes

Leaves from 1 bunch fresh
parsley, chopped

Leaves from 1 bunch fresh
cilantro, chopped

Leaves from 1 bunch fresh
basil, chopped

2 tablespoons / 28 grams
fish sauce

SCALLOPS

16 U-10 dry packed **scallops**

2¼ cups / 500 grams **water**

1¾ tablepoons / 25 grams
fine sea salt, plus more for
seasoning

3 tablespoons / 45 grams
olive oil

3 tablespoons / 45 grams
unsalted butter

In a large sauté pan, heat the olive oil over high heat. If you do not have a pan large enough to cook all of the scallops, cook them in two pans. Remove the scallops from the refrigerator, pat them dry, and season them with salt. When the oil begins to shimmer, add the scallops to the pan. Once the scallops are in the pan, turn the heat down to medium-high. A crust will start to form on the bottom of the scallops after 3 to 5 minutes. At this point, flip the scallops, add the butter to the pan, and use a large spoon to baste the scallops as they cook. Turn the heat down if the butter starts to brown. Once the bottoms are golden brown, about 2 minutes, flip them over and continue to baste the scallops for another minute.

Remove the scallops from the pan and put them on a plate in a warm place. Put the green sauce in a small pot set over medium heat and bring to a simmer. Remove the pot from the heat.

To serve, put the green sauce and 2 scallops on each of 8 plates and spoon the plate juices over the top.

SOAKING THE SCALLOPS; DRY THEM COMPLETELY BEFORE COOKING

138

FISH TACOS DONE RIGHT ARE HARD TO BEAT. HERE WE MAKE
a seasoning blend and mix it with olive oil to brush on the fish
before marinating. It adds flavor to the dish, as the spices toast
when you grill the fish, and the oil keeps the fish from sticking
to the grill. A cool, fresh tomato-avocado salad and shredded
cabbage make great complements to warm fish in a great
homemade tortilla.

MAKES 8 TACOS

FISH TACOS

Cut the fish into eight 2-ounce (57-gram) portions, checking to be sure
there are no remaining bones, and put the fish in a baking dish. In a
small bowl, combine the garlic powder, onion powder, ancho powder,
½ teaspoon (3 grams) salt, and olive oil and use a pastry brush to mix
together. Brush the mixture generously over the fish so that each piece is
well coated.

In a large bowl, combine the tomatoes, scallions, jalapeño,
avocados, and lime juice. Mix gently and add salt to taste. Put the cabbage
in a serving bowl and season lightly with salt (0.5%). Put the cilantro
leaves in a separate serving bowl.

Preheat a grill to medium-high heat (400°F/205°C). Grill the fish
for 30 seconds on each side, and then turn the pieces of fish 90 degrees
and cook for an additional 30 seconds on each side so that it is nicely
crosshatched and just cooked through. Transfer to a large plate. Grill
the tortillas lightly on both sides, so that they are marked and warmed
through but still flexible. Stack them on a plate and cover them with a
clean, damp linen napkin or towel.

Serve the fish, tortillas, tomato-avocado salad, cabbage, cilantro,
lime quarters, and sour cream so that people can build their own tacos.

1 pound / 455 grams **white flaky fish fillets,** such as mahimahi

½ teaspoon / 1 gram **garlic powder**

½ teaspoon / 1 gram **onion powder**

¼ teaspoon / 0.5 gram **ancho chile powder** or other mild chile powder

½ teaspoon / 3 grams **fine sea salt,** plus more for seasoning

2 tablespoons / 28 grams **olive oil**

3 large **tomatoes,** chopped

3 **scallions,** sliced

1 medium **jalapeño,** seeded and finely chopped

2 **avocados,** chopped

Juice of 2 **limes,** plus 2 limes, quartered

¼ head **red cabbage,** shredded

1 cup / 18 grams fresh **cilantro leaves**

8 **Smoked Tortillas** (recipe follows)

1 cup / 240 grams **sour cream** or Toasted Coconut Crème Fraîche (page 240)

SMOKED TORTILLAS

We love tortillas, but we always get caught in the endless debate of flour versus corn. This recipe brings both flours together for the best of both worlds—including smoking the masa corn flour for an added layer of flavor. The perfect balance of flavor and texture, these tortillas are pliable enough to wrap around a filling without breaking but have that nutty corn taste and feel. We usually eat at least one straight from the pan just because they taste so good.

1 cup / 150 grams **instant masa harina**

1 cup / 150 grams **all-purpose flour**

1 teaspoon / 6 grams **baking powder**

¾ teaspoon / 4.5 grams **fine sea salt**

1 teaspoon / 5 grams **bacon fat**, at room temperature, or canola oil

¾ cup / 170 grams **water**

¼ cup / 65 grams **whole milk**

Cold smoke the masa harina for 45 to 60 minutes (see page 120).

In a medium bowl, whisk together the masa harina, all-purpose flour, baking powder, and salt. Make a well in the center. In a microwave-safe 2-cup measuring cup, combine the bacon fat, water, and milk and microwave on high for 45 seconds until the liquid is warm and the bacon fat has melted. Pour the liquid into the flour mixture and use your fingers or a rubber spatula to stir together, starting from the inside and working your way outward. Once it begins to come together into a soft dough, turn it out onto a clean countertop and begin to work the flour still remaining in the bowl into the dough. Add an extra tablespoon or two of water if necessary to form a soft, pliable dough. Knead the dough a few times, then wrap it in plastic wrap, and let it rest at room temperature for 30 minutes.

Heat a cast-iron skillet or griddle over medium heat. Divide the dough into 10 equal portions and roll each portion into a ball. Roll out the first ball on a well-floured surface until it is about ⅛ inch (3 mm) thick. Put it into the hot skillet and let it cook while you roll out the next tortilla. (Alternatively, you can roll out and stack all of the tortillas, putting a piece of parchment or wax paper between each one before cooking. If you do it this way, be sure to keep them covered with a towel or plastic wrap so they don't dry out.)

Once the tortilla begins to bubble and has turned a light golden brown on the bottom, 30 to 45 seconds, flip it and cook the other side until it is a pale golden brown, 30 to 45 seconds more. Transfer the tortilla to a tortilla warmer or a basket lined with a cloth napkin to stay warm and immediately add the next tortilla to the skillet, adjusting the heat slightly if the pan starts to get too hot. Continue to cook and stack the tortillas until they are all finished. Once cool, the tortillas can be kept in a zip-top bag at room temperature for up to 5 days.

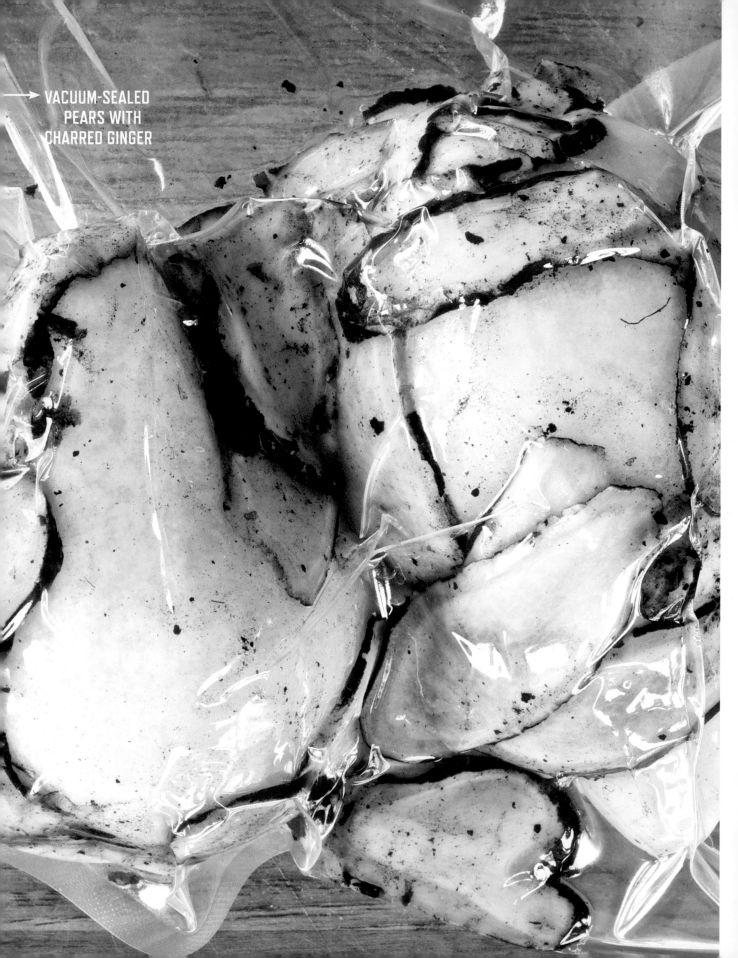

VACUUM-SEALED
PEARS WITH
CHARRED GINGER

GINGER
SCALLION SQUID

CALAMARI IS ONE OF THOSE INGREDIENTS THAT REQUIRE EITHER quick cooking or long, slow cooking if it is to emerge tender, not rubbery. The key technique in this recipe is quickly cooking the squid sous vide at 162°F (72°C) to give it a silky texture with a hint of chew. The water bath is also ideal for cooking the pears and infusing them with ginger. The final step of charring the ginger adds flavor without compromising the texture. This is a wonderful chilled seafood salad with a range of textures and flavors, none of them rubbery.

SERVES 8 AS AN APPETIZER

GINGER SCALLION SQUID

Preheat a circulating water bath or large pot of water to 162°F (72°C); see page 180.

Put the water and salt in a large bowl and stir to dissolve the salt. Put the squid into the brine and refrigerate for 10 minutes. Remove the squid from the brine and divide it between 2 vacuum bags—the bodies in one bag and the tentacles in another—and seal, or alternatively, put them into 2 zip-top bags, remove the air, and seal. Cook in the water bath or stockpot for 10 minutes. Transfer the bags to an ice water bath and let cool.

Increase the temperature of the circulating water bath to 181°F (83°C).

Meanwhile, put the ginger on a wire rack set over a baking sheet and put it on top of the stove. Use a butane torch to completely char the exterior of the ginger on both sides. Let the ginger cool and then use a mandoline or sharp knife to thinly slice it.

Peel the pears and put 2 pears in each of 2 vacuum bags. Divide the ginger between the bags, covering the pears with the slices. Vacuum-seal the bags, or alternatively, put the pears and ginger into 2 zip-top bags, remove the air, and seal. Cook in the water bath or stockpot for 55 minutes. Transfer the bags to an ice water bath. Once completely cool—after about 30 minutes—put the pears in their bags in the refrigerator until ready to serve.

4½ cups / 1,000 grams **water**

8 teaspoons / 50 grams **fine sea salt**

2 pounds / 875 grams **cleaned large squid**

3.5 ounces / 100 grams peeled **fresh ginger**

2¼ pounds / 1,028 grams **Bosc pears** (4 medium)

1¼ cups / 150 grams **pistachios**, roasted (see page 39)

¼ teaspoon / 1.5 grams **smoked salt**

0.4 ounce / 12 grams **palm sugar**, grated on a box grater, or 4 teaspoons packed dark brown sugar

Grated zest of 2 **limes**

¼ teaspoon / 0.5 gram **jalapeño powder** or cayenne pepper

In a food processor, combine the pistachios, smoked salt, palm sugar, lime zest, and jalapeño powder. Pulse the ingredients until they form a small uniform crumb. Do not process continuously because you don't want to make a pistachio paste. Reserve in a zip-top bag or a covered container.

When you're ready to serve, slice the scallions into ⅛-inch-thick (3 mm) slices. Put the honey, vinegar, soy sauce, and ½ teaspoon (3 grams) salt into a bowl and stir to dissolve the salt. Add the scallions and stir to coat. Cut the pear bags open and pour any juices into the bowl. Add the olive oil and stir to combine.

Cut each pear lengthwise into eighths. Use a paring knife to remove the core and seeds from each piece. Slice each piece of pear crosswise into ¼-inch-thick (6 mm) slices. Add the pears to the bowl with the scallion dressing and stir to combine.

Cut open the bags of squid and pour off the liquid. Slice the squid bodies into ¼-inch (6 mm) rings and separate the tentacles into individual legs. Add them to the bowl with the pears and stir to combine. Spoon the mixture into 8 small bowls and sprinkle the pistachio mixture on top. Serve immediately.

8 scallions

½ tablespoon / 8 grams **honey**

1½ tablespoons / 21 grams **rice vinegar**

2 teaspoons / 10 grams **tamari soy sauce**

½ teaspoon / 3 grams **fine sea salt**

¼ cup / 56 grams **extra-virgin olive oil** or **pistachio oil**

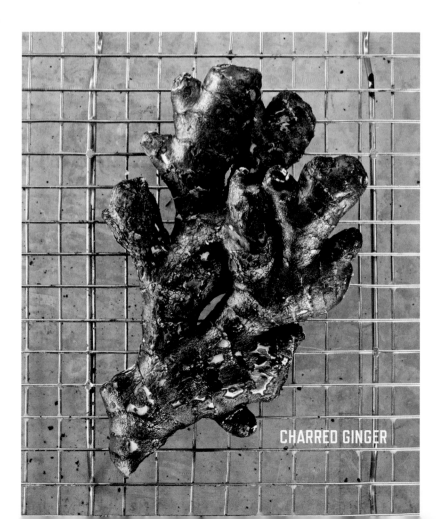

CHARRED GINGER

JUST FIVE INGREDIENTS COMBINE IN THIS RECIPE FOR A
delicious weeknight dish that will forever banish overcooked,
bland fish from your dinner table. The bold flavors of this
glaze are the perfect foil to the meaty texture of salmon, which
caramelizes under the broiler and then finishes cooking while
the oven cools. The resulting fish has a firm exterior giving way
to moist, tender, silky flesh. It's delicious paired with Grilled
Leeks Vinaigrette (page 87) or a perfect Potato Gratin (page 121).

SERVES 4

SMOKED MAPLE &
MISO GLAZED
WILD ALASKAN SALMON

¼ cup / 70 grams **white miso**

¼ cup / 60 grams **maple syrup**

1 tablespoon / 14 grams **sherry vinegar**

½ teaspoon / 1 gram **smoked hot paprika**

4 (6-ounce / 170-gram) **wild Alaskan salmon fillets**

In a small bowl, whisk together the miso, maple syrup, vinegar, and
paprika. Brush the marinade on the fish, put the fish on a plate, cover
with plastic wrap, and let rest in the refrigerator for 4 hours.

Preheat the broiler to high. Line a baking sheet with foil.

Lay the fish on the baking sheet, leaving 2 inches (5 cm) of space
between each piece. Broil for 5 minutes, positioning the fish about
4 inches (10 cm) from the heat source, until the top is just starting to
brown. Turn off the broiler and remove the pan from the oven. Let the
fish rest for 10 minutes in a warm spot on top of the stove. It will finish
cooking as it rests.

THE WARM MOIST HEAT OF A STEAMER IS WONDERFUL FOR keeping fish juicy. If we happen to have some leftover herb stems or aromatics, we happily add them to the steaming liquid. Layering flavors in a dish is our favorite way to amplify flavor. Here coconut is the star player and we've used it in a variety of ways. Coconut oil adds nutty notes and richness to the halibut and Thai basil imparts its spicy flavor as it cooks. The coconut pesto is a twist on another classic preparation; blanching the basil means you can make the sauce in advance without fear of oxidation. Finally the toasted coconut seasoning added at the end gives the dish texture and a hint of crunch.

SERVES 6

COCONUT STEAMED HALIBUT

PREPARE THE HALIBUT: Cut the halibut into 6 equal pieces. Put the water and salt into a large bowl and stir to dissolve the salt. Put the halibut into the brine for 10 minutes. Remove the fish from the brine and pat it dry.

Put the coconut oil in a microwave-safe bowl and microwave for 30 seconds until it is just melted. Put a 12-inch (30 cm) square of plastic wrap on the counter. Put a piece of halibut in the center of the plastic wrap. Brush coconut oil onto the halibut and then put a sprig of Thai basil on top. Brush the halibut with the coconut oil again. Wrap the halibut in the plastic wrap and repeat with the remaining pieces. Refrigerate for at least 4 hours and up to 24 hours.

Preheat the oven to 350°F (175°C). Line a baking sheet with parchment paper.

MAKE THE COCONUT PESTO: In a medium bowl, stir together the coconut flakes, sugar, ⅛ teaspoon (0.75 gram) of the salt, the cumin, cinnamon, and garlic powder. Transfer to the baking sheet and bake until the flakes are golden brown, 4 to 5 minutes. Remove the baking sheet from the oven, stir the coconut, and let cool.

HALIBUT

2 pounds / 910 grams skin-on **halibut fillet**

4½ cups / 1,000 grams **water**

2 tablespoons plus 2 teaspoons / 50 grams **fine sea salt**

3 tablespoons plus 2 teaspoons / 50 grams **virgin coconut oil**

6 sprigs fresh **Thai basil** or regular basil

COCONUT PESTO

1½ cups / 80 grams large **unsweetened coconut flakes**

1 teaspoon / 4 grams **sugar**

⅜ teaspoon / 2.25 grams **fine sea salt**

⅛ teaspoon / 0.3 gram **ground cumin**

⅛ teaspoon / 0.15 gram **ground cinnamon**

⅛ teaspoon / 0.4 gram **garlic powder**

6 cups / 113 grams fresh **basil leaves**

¼ cup / 120 grams **cold water**

7 tablespoons plus 2 teaspoons / 100 grams **virgin coconut oil**

Transfer the toasted coconut to a pan in an outdoor or stovetop smoker and smoke for 15 minutes (see page 120). Remove the flakes from the smoker and let cool. Put the coconut in a zip-top bag until ready to use, or for up to 3 days.

Bring a medium pot of water to a boil over high heat. Blanch the basil leaves for 30 seconds, working with about one-third at a time, and transfer to an ice water bath. Drain the basil and squeeze it dry. Put the basil, 1 cup (53 grams) of the smoked toasted coconut flakes, the water, coconut oil, and remaining ¼ teaspoon (1.5 grams) salt into a blender. Turn the blender on low and increase the speed to medium. Blend for 1 minute. Turn off the blender and scrape down the sides. Turn the blender back on, increase the speed to high, and puree until the mixture is completely smooth, about 1 minute. Transfer the pesto to a covered container and store in the refrigerator until ready to use (up to 24 hours).

Put 2 inches (5 cm) of water into a large steamer set over high heat. When the water is boiling, unwrap the halibut and put the fish into the steamer. Turn the heat down to medium-high and steam the fish for 5 minutes. Turn the steamer off and let the fish steam for 2 more minutes.

Remove the fish from the steamer and set on a clean plate. Put the coconut pesto into a small saucepan and gently warm it over medium heat to just melt the coconut oil. Gently lift the skin off the fish and put the fish on each of 6 plates. Top with some of the coconut pesto and then sprinkle with the remaining ½ cup (26 grams) smoked toasted coconut flakes.

PESTO is a classic Italian sauce, commonly associated with Genoa. Traditionally it is made with fresh basil, garlic, pine nuts, olive oil and hard cheeses, like Parmigiano Reggiano and Fiore Sardo. It was originally made in a mortar and pestle and the ingredients were ground together to make an aromatic sauce. These days pesto has developed a more elastic description. Creative cooks vary the type of herb, nuts, cheeses, and even the oil used to make the sauce. The results, while in no way authentic, are still delicious. It's the American way to mix and match to make things our own and that is fine as long as in the end it still makes for a great meal.

POULTRY & MEAT

WE ARE PASSIONATE ABOUT PIE, SO WHEN IT CAME TO MAKING a great chicken pie, we wanted one where the meat was still juicy and the vegetables were tender but still distinct and flavorful. The best chicken pie must be made with savory pie dough and meaty gravy that keeps everything moist. Whole chicken thighs are juicy and flavorful and we make a pressure-cooked broth using the skin and bones for the gravy. Nothing goes to waste and the finished pie is close to perfect.

SERVES 6

CHICKEN PIE

PREPARE THE CHICKEN: Skin the thighs and cut out the bones; set the skin and bones aside. Cut the meat of each thigh in half and then cut each half into thirds. Put the chicken meat in a small bowl, add the tapioca starch and ½ teaspoon (3 grams) of the salt, and mix gently to combine. Cover and reserve in the refrigerator for the filling.

MAKE THE BROTH: Put the reserved skin and bones in a pressure cooker with the onion, garlic, soy sauce, water, and remaining ¼ teaspoon (1.5 grams) salt. Cook at high pressure for 30 minutes. Let the pressure dissipate naturally. Strain the chicken broth into a bowl and cool it over an ice water bath. Measure out 1 cup for the gravy. Freeze the remainder for another use.

MAKE THE PIE CRUST: In a food processor, combine the flour, salt, sugar, garlic powder, and onion powder and pulse 4 or 5 times to blend. Add the butter and pulse 2 or 3 times to blend. Pour the ice water into the food processor and run the processor for 5 to 10 seconds to bring the mixture together. If it seems a little dry, add more water 1 tablespoon at a time. The dough will resemble small pebbles and hold together when you squeeze a bit in your hand. Turn the dough out onto a floured countertop. Sprinkle the dough lightly with flour. Starting at one end, use the heel of your hand to smear the dough into the counter in small amounts. Do this quickly, being sure not to work any section of dough more than once. This technique, known as fraisage, forms flaky layers of fat and flour. Use a bench scraper or spatula to remove the pieces of dough from the countertop. Gently press them into 2 compact balls of dough and flatten into discs, one slightly larger than the other, each no more than 2 inches

(recipe continues)

CHICKEN AND BROTH

2¼ pounds / 1,020 grams bone-in, skin-on **chicken thighs** (about 6 large)

¼ cup / 24 grams **tapioca starch**

¾ teaspoon / 4.5 grams **fine sea salt**

1 medium **onion,** diced

2 **garlic** cloves, crushed

¼ cup / 65 grams **tamari soy sauce**

2 cups / 450 grams **water**

PIE CRUST

2¼ cups / 337.5 grams **all-purpose flour**

1 teaspoon / 6 grams **fine sea salt**

1 teaspoon / 4 grams **sugar**

½ teaspoon / 1 gram **garlic powder**

½ teaspoon / 1 gram **onion powder**

8 ounces / 225 grams cold **unsalted butter,** diced

½ cup / 113 grams **ice water**

(5 cm) thick. You can roll them out and use immediately or freeze for up to 1 month; alternatively, the dough can be wrapped in plastic wrap and refrigerated for up to 1 week. Let the refrigerated dough rest at room temperature for at least 30 minutes before rolling.

Roll out the larger piece of dough into a circle with a diameter of 12 inches (30 cm) and that's about ¼ inch (6 mm) thick, and fit it into a 9-inch (23 cm) deep-dish pie pan. Trim the overhang to 1 inch (2.5 cm) past the edge of the pie pan. Put the pie pan in the freezer while you prepare the filling. Roll the smaller half out into a round about ¼ inch (6 mm) thick. Set it on a parchment paper— or plastic wrap—lined baking sheet, cover with plastic wrap, and put in the refrigerator until you are ready to use it.

Preheat the oven to 400°F (205°C).

MAKE THE FILLING: Put 2 inches (5 cm) of water into a large steamer set over high heat. When the water is boiling, steam the potatoes until they are just tender and cooked through, 10 to 12 minutes. Remove them from the steamer and let cool slightly.

Put the 1 cup reserved cold chicken broth in a medium saucepan. Add the cornstarch and whisk to combine. Bring to a boil over medium-high heat and cook, stirring constantly, until the broth has thickened. Set the pot in an ice water bath to cool the broth, stirring occasionally.

Meanwhile, set a large sauté pan over medium-high heat and add 1 tablespoon (14 grams) of the olive oil. Once the oil has begun to shimmer, add the onion and sauté until golden brown, 4 to 5 minutes. Transfer the onion to a medium bowl and return the sauté pan to the heat. Add the remaining 1 tablespoon (14 grams) oil and when it begins to shimmer, add the carrots and celery and sauté until translucent and just tender, 3 to 4 minutes. Add to the onions.

While the vegetables cool, use a paring knife to peel the potatoes and cut them into 1-inch (2.5 cm) pieces. Add the potatoes and the peas to the bowl and season the vegetables lightly with salt. Add the starch-coated chicken pieces to the bowl, discarding any excess starch left behind. Add the cooled broth and fold everything together.

Fill the bottom crust of the pie with the chicken mixture and then cover with the top crust, pressing the edges together and tucking them underneath the edge of the pie pan. Gently crimp the edges together. Brush the pie with the milk. Sprinkle fleur de sel and cracked black pepper over the top. Cut a vent in the center of the pie.

Bake for 30 minutes, reduce the temperature to 350°F (175°C), and bake until the crust is a deep golden brown, about 1 more hour. Remove from the oven and let rest for 10 minutes before serving.

PIE FILLING

2 large **russet potatoes**

2 tablespoons / 14 grams **cornstarch**

2 tablespoons / 28 grams **olive oil**

1 medium **onion,** chopped

3 medium **carrots,** cut into ½-inch / 13 mm pieces

3 medium **celery ribs,** cut into ½-inch / 13 mm pieces

½ cup / 70 grams **frozen green peas,** thawed

Fine sea salt

1 tablespoon / 16 grams **whole milk**

Fleur de sel

Black pepper

BAKING SODA

This unassuming ingredient is in every kitchen and has an astonishing number of uses. Baking soda, or pure sodium bicarbonate, is a naturally occurring alkaline ingredient that is ground to a fine powder for household use. You can keep boxes of it in the refrigerator to absorb odors and add it to the washing machine to soften water and remove odors from clothes. We like to use it to scrub pots and pans, as it does an effective job of breaking down cooked-on food and is gentle on our cookware.

Baking soda is most commonly thought of as a baking ingredient, because when you combine it with heat or a weak acid it forms carbon dioxide, which helps aerate batters and quick breads. This leavening action is also employed when making nut and seed brittles to create a fine network of holes in the finished candy that results in its brittle texture. Baking soda is used in larger quantities in some cookie doughs to weaken gluten, which means that more moisture can escape during the baking process and the cookies will collapse after rising to create a thin, crisp cookie with a fine, brittle texture that is easy to bite through.

Baking soda blended with an acid makes baking powder. Commercial baking powders are designed to be double acting so that leavening occurs twice, once upon the addition of liquids and again in the presence of heat. Combining 1 part baking soda with 2 parts cream of tartar makes homemade single-action baking powder.

Baking soda is used to add alkalinity to bread and pasta dough. Baking soda or baking powder is kneaded into steamed bun dough after the initial rise in order to neutralize the acids created through fermentation. This step helps soften the texture of the dough, which in turn allows it to rise more smoothly in the steamer. It's an interesting sensation to knead baking soda into dough and feel it stiffen under your hands—and then to steam it and bite into the tender, yet firm, bun.

A similar thing happens when we add baking soda to our noodle dough to firm up the texture. Gluten formation is maximized at a slightly acidic pH, ranging from 5 to 6. Anything above or below that pH will reduce gluten strength. This neutralization of the dough is what gives ramen noodles their bouncy, yet tender, texture. Adding baking soda inhibits the noodles' ability to absorb water by stiffening the cell walls and making them less permeable, which is beneficial because it makes it harder to overcook noodles.

Traditionally baking soda was added to vegetables to help them retain their bright colors during long boiling periods. While long-cooked vegetables are no longer in fashion, baking soda is still used in the savory kitchen to tenderize meat before stir-frying. It works by raising the pH of the surface layer of the meat and activating enzymes, called calpains, which begin to break down the muscle fibers. This process softens the texture of the cooked meat and allows it to retain moisture. We also use a small amount of baking soda in our roasted chicken wings to promote deep, even browning and a thin, crisp skin. The alkaline effect of the baking soda helps speed up the Maillard reaction, or browning, when the wings cook. The trick is to use just enough, because too much baking soda can add a slightly bitter, mineral taste to your food. When used judiciously, it disappears into the natural flavor of your food.

OUR SIMPLE TRICK FOR THE BEST KOREAN-STYLE WINGS IS TO marinate the wings in a mixture of egg whites, salt, and baking soda. This forms an even coating that clings to the wings and seasons them. The mixture also helps to break down the outer layer of proteins on the skin, allowing the chicken to render and brown in the oven and resulting in juicy wings with a thin, crackling skin. (You can also brush the marinade on a whole chicken before roasting.) We've paired the wings with yangnyeomjang, a spicy Korean dipping sauce, to accent the sweet flavor of the chicken.

SERVES 4 TO 6

KOREAN-STYLE CHICKEN WINGS

Put the egg whites, baking soda, and salt in a bowl and stir to dissolve the salt and baking soda. Add the chicken wings and stir to coat evenly. Remove the wings from the bowl and lay them out on 2 wire racks, each set over a baking sheet. Refrigerate the wings uncovered overnight for them to dry out.

Preheat the oven to 450°F (235°C).

Put the wings, still on the racks on the baking sheets, into the oven and cook for 15 minutes. Flip the wings over and bake for 10 minutes. Flip the wings over again and bake until a deep golden brown with a crackling skin, about 10 more minutes. Take the pans out of the oven and let cool for 5 minutes.

Meanwhile, in a small bowl, combine the soy sauce, apple juice, honey, rice vinegar, sesame oil, chile flakes, sesame seeds, garlic, ginger, and scallion.

Pile the wings on a serving platter and serve the sauce alongside.

3 large **egg whites**

2 teaspoons / 10 grams **baking soda**

1¾ teaspoons / 10.5 grams **fine sea salt**

4 pounds / 1.8 kilograms whole **chicken wings**

¼ cup / 65 grams **tamari soy sauce**

3 tablespoons / 42 grams **apple juice**

1 tablespoon / 16 grams **honey**

1 tablespoon / 14 grams **rice vinegar**

1 tablespoon / 14 grams **toasted sesame oil**

1 teaspoons / 2 grams **Korean red chile flakes**

1 tablespoon / 3.75 grams **toasted sesame seeds,** chopped

1 **garlic** clove, grated

½ teaspoon / 2.5 grams grated **fresh ginger**

1 **scallion,** finely sliced

THOUGH IT REQUIRES A LITTLE ADVANCE PLANNING, BECAUSE the chicken needs to brine overnight, this recipe makes a great go-to weeknight dinner. The lemony brine has a blend of spices to create a tart, spicy seasoning. The thighs are pulled out of the brine, rolled in seasoned bread crumbs (which can also be made in advance), and put into the oven. They get rotated once during cooking, leaving you plenty of time to sauté some vegetables or toss a salad to serve alongside. The chicken emerges from the oven crisp and juicy; it's almost impossible to eat just one piece.

SERVES 4 TO 6

OVEN-FRIED LEMON CHICKEN

CHICKEN

2 cups / 480 grams **whey (page 55)** or cultured buttermilk, homemade (page 54) or store-bought

2 tablespoons / 33 grams **tamari soy sauce**

1 teaspoon / 6 grams **fine sea salt**

½ teaspoon / 1 gram **garlic powder**

½ teaspoon / 1 gram **onion powder**

¼ teaspoon / 1 gram **Boyajian lemon oil** or lemon essential oil or grated zest from 2 lemons

¼ teaspoon / 0.5 gram **ground cumin**

⅛ teaspoon / 0.25 gram **cayenne pepper**

4 pounds / 1.8 kilograms bone-in, skin-on **chicken thighs** (10 to 12 large)

BRINE THE CHICKEN: In a large bowl, whisk together the whey, soy sauce, salt, garlic powder, onion powder, lemon oil, cumin, and cayenne. Add the chicken thighs and stir gently to coat them. Cover with plastic wrap or transfer to a lidded container and refrigerate for at least 8 hours and up to 24 hours.

Preheat the oven to 450°F (235°C). Put a large rimmed baking sheet—big enough to hold all of the chicken in a single layer—in the oven to preheat.

MAKE THE BREAD CRUMBS: In a medium bowl, combine the bread crumbs, Parmigiano, garlic powder, onion powder, paprika, cayenne, and salt and whisk to blend.

Drain the chicken, discarding the brine. Set the chicken next to the bowl of bread crumbs and a large baking sheet on the other side. Take one piece of chicken, still damp from the brine, and put it in the bowl of crumbs. Turn it over a few times to coat it thoroughly, then gently shake off any excess crumbs, and transfer it to the baking sheet. Repeat with the remaining chicken.

Once all of the chicken has been coated and the oven is hot, remove the baking sheet from the oven. Add the butter to the baking sheet and swirl the pan so the butter coats the bottom. Immediately add the chicken thighs, setting them skin side down, and put the pan in the oven. Lower the oven temperature to 400°F (205°C) and cook for 20 minutes. Flip over the chicken pieces and bake until golden brown and the meat is starting to pull back from the tips of the bones, about 20 more minutes. Remove the pan from the oven and let the chicken rest on the baking pan for 10 minutes before serving.

BREAD CRUMBS

About 2 cups / 250 grams **dried bread crumbs**

2 tablespoons / 10 grams freshly grated **Parmigiano Reggiano cheese**

½ teaspoon / 1 gram **garlic powder**

½ teaspoon / 1 gram **onion powder**

½ teaspoon / 1 gram **sweet Spanish paprika**

¼ teaspoon / 0.5 gram **cayenne pepper**

¼ teaspoon / 1.5 grams **fine sea salt**

4 tablespoons / 56 grams **unsalted butter,** diced

WE LOVE CHINESE FOOD, BUT UNFORTUNATELY, IT'S HARD TO come by good Chinese food where we live. So we began making our own. The downside to classic General Tso's is that it tends to be too sweet, oversauced, and light on the broccoli. We wanted to transform the dish into something a little more balanced. This recipe utilizes the tastiest part of the chicken: the thighs. We usually buy family-size packages of free-range thighs, cut them up, and use the skins and the bones for the sauce and the meat for the dish. This recipe looks like a lot of work, but don't let that deter you. Some of the steps can be done the day before, and all of them are relatively simple. All you'll need for serving is some steamed rice.

SERVES 6

GENERAL TSO'S CHICKEN

CHICKEN

3 large **egg whites**

5 tablespoons / 82 grams **tamari soy sauce**

2 tablespoons / 28 grams **rice vinegar**

2½ pounds / 1.2 kilograms bone-in, skin-on **chicken thighs** (8 to 10)

3⅓ cups / 750 grams **water**

1 **star anise**

1 **cinnamon stick**

½ ounce / 15 grams peeled **fresh ginger**

2 cups / 224 grams **cornstarch,** for coating

Rice bran oil or peanut oil, for frying

PREPARE THE CHICKEN: In a medium bowl, whisk together the egg whites, 2 tablespoons (33 grams) of the tamari, and the vinegar and set the bowl beside your cutting board. Remove the skins from the chicken thighs and put them in the bowl of a pressure cooker. Use a sharp paring knife to remove the bones from each thigh, trimming away any small chunks of fat or bits of sinew; put the bones, fat, and sinew in the pressure cooker. Cut each piece of thigh meat into thirds and put them in the bowl of marinade. Cover the marinating thigh meat and refrigerate for at least 4 hours and up to 24 hours.

Add the water, remaining 3 tablespoons (49 grams) tamari, the star anise, cinnamon, and ginger to the pressure cooker and cook at high pressure for 30 minutes. Let the pressure dissipate naturally. Alternatively, you can combine the ingredients in a large pot set over medium heat. Bring it to a simmer and cook for 2 hours, skimming the top occasionally. Turn off the heat and let the broth cool to room temperature. Skim it and strain it through a fine-mesh sieve; discard the solids. Chill the broth, uncovered, in the refrigerator until completely cold, about 4 hours. You will need 2 cups (450 grams) for the sauce. The remaining broth can be covered and kept in the refrigerator for up to 5 days. Any fat that solidifies on top can be scraped off and stored in the refrigerator for cooking.

Put a baking sheet with a wire rack over it near the stove. Drain the marinade off the chicken and put the cornstarch in a medium bowl. Add a couple of pieces of chicken at a time to the cornstarch and coat them well. Shake off any excess cornstarch and put the thighs on a separate baking sheet. Repeat until all of the chicken is coated.

Pour 3 inches (8 cm) of oil into a pot and heat to 375°F (190°C). Working in batches, fry the chicken until golden brown and just cooked through, 2 to 3 minutes. Transfer to the wire rack and let rest.

MAKE THE SAUCE: In a large sauté pan or deep skillet, combine the reserved 2 cups (450 grams) chicken broth, tamari, pickled ginger juice, vinegar, hoisin sauce, marmalade, sesame oil, Sriracha sauce, garlic powder, and cornstarch and whisk to blend. Set the pan over medium-high heat and stir constantly until the mixture comes to a simmer and begins to thicken, about 5 minutes. Continue to cook for 2 to 3 minutes until the sauce has thickened and becomes glossy.

Meanwhile, microwave the broccoli for 4 to 5 minutes on high until it is just tender.

Add the chicken and broccoli to the sauce and toss gently to coat. Transfer to a large serving bowl and serve hot.

SAUCE

2 tablespoons / 33 grams **tamari soy sauce**

2 tablespoons / 32 grams **pickled ginger juice** (from a jar of pickled ginger)

2 tablespoons / 28 grams **rice vinegar**

4 teaspoons / 20 grams **hoisin sauce**

4 teaspoons / 24 grams **Meyer Lemon Marmalade** (page 237) or orange marmalade

4 teaspoons / 20 grams **sesame oil**

2 teaspoons / 10 grams **Sriracha sauce**

1 teaspoon / 2 grams **garlic powder**

4 tablespoons / 28 grams **cornstarch**

1 bunch **broccoli,** cut into bite-size pieces

THESE RIBS ARE WRAPPED IN LAYERS OF PARCHMENT AND FOIL and then slow-roasted in a low oven until the meat falls off the bone. The moist heat yields incredibly succulent meat that is fork-tender and finger-licking good. What's nice is that once you put the ribs in the oven you can pretty much forget about them, and a few hours later you will have a wonderful main course almost ready to go. These are delicious with Kale Slaw (page 95) or Lemon Roasted Potatoes (page 125). The ginger ketchup for the ribs is an Asian-style barbecue sauce, and leftovers are delicious on burgers, brushed onto grilled chicken legs, or anywhere else you enjoy using traditional barbecue sauce.

SERVES 4

CHINESE SPARERIBS

PREPARE THE RIBS: In a small bowl, combine the salt, sugar, garlic powder, chile powder, cinnamon, ginger, cloves, mace, and soy sauce and stir to combine. Remove the membrane from the back of the ribs and then use a pastry brush to apply the paste over the entire rack. Wrap the ribs in plastic wrap and refrigerate overnight.

MAKE THE GINGER KETCHUP: In a small saucepan, combine the red wine vinegar, soy sauce, and balsamic vinegar. Bring the mixture to a simmer over low heat and cook until it has reduced by two-thirds, about 15 minutes. Pour the reduced syrup into a blender and add the pickled ginger with its juice and the ketchup. Turn the blender on low and increase the speed to high. Puree the mixture until it is smooth. Strain the ginger ketchup through a fine-mesh sieve, let cool, and reserve in a covered container in the refrigerator.

Preheat the oven to 250°F (120°C).

(recipe continues)

RIBS

1½ teaspoons / 9 grams **fine sea salt**

1 teaspoon / 4 grams **sugar**

½ teaspoon / 1 gram **garlic powder**

¼ teaspoon / 0.5 gram **ancho chile powder**

¼ teaspoon / 0.5 gram **ground cinnamon**

¼ teaspoon / 0.5 gram **ground ginger**

⅛ teaspoon / 0.25 gram **ground cloves**

⅛ teaspoon / 0.25 gram **ground mace**

1 tablespoon / 16 grams **tamari soy sauce**

1 full rack **St. Louis cut pork spareribs** (2½ pounds / 1.150 kilograms)

GINGER KETCHUP

7½ tablespoons / 105 grams **red wine vinegar**

6½ tablespoons / 105 grams **tamari soy sauce**

7½ tablespoons / 105 grams **balsamic vinegar**

7 tablespoons / 105 grams **pickled ginger**

1 cup plus 2 tablespoons / 300 grams **ketchup**

Remove the ribs from the refrigerator and take off the plastic wrap. Lay the ribs on a piece of parchment paper, cover with another piece of parchment paper, and crimp the edges all the way around to form a closed package. Put the parchment-wrapped meat on a large piece of foil. Top the packet with another piece of foil and crimp the edges all the way around to seal the package. Put the ribs on a large baking sheet and bake for 4 hours.

Preheat the broiler.

Take the ribs out of the oven and let them rest for 10 minutes. Take them out of their packaging and transfer them, meat side up, to a wire rack set over a baking sheet. Brush the ribs with an even layer of the ginger ketchup and broil 4 to 6 inches (10 to 15 cm) from the heat source for 5 minutes so that the ketchup caramelizes and the top of the ribs gets crispy.

Remove the pan from the oven and put the ribs on a cutting board. Use scissors to cut them into pairs or individual ribs and put them on a platter. Serve with ginger ketchup on the side.

LAMB SHOULDER IS PERCEIVED AS A TOUGH CUT OF MEAT, but it can be very tender. We marinate it overnight and then slow-cook it in the oven until you can pull it apart with a fork. It takes an inexpensive cut of meat and turns it into a centerpiece for the table. Garnished with a tangy smoked raisin relish, this underutilized cut of meat becomes something to remember.

SERVES 8

SLOW-ROASTED LAMB SHOULDER
WITH SMOKED RAISIN RELISH

MAKE THE SMOKED RAISIN RELISH: Put the raisins in a pan that fits into a stovetop or outdoor smoker. Cold smoke for 1 hour (see page 120).

In a bowl, combine the grape juice, honey, vinegar, and salt and stir to combine and dissolve the salt. Add the smoked raisins to the bowl and stir. Put the raisin mixture into a covered container and refrigerate for at least 2 days to hydrate the raisins and allow the flavors to blend. The relish will keep for up to 2 weeks in the refrigerator.

PREPARE THE LAMB SHOULDER: In a large bowl (big enough to hold the lamb shoulder), combine the brown sugar, red wine, soy sauce, smoked paprika, cumin, and salt and whisk together into a loose paste. Put the lamb shoulder in the bowl and evenly coat it with the paste. Lay two sheets of plastic wrap, roughly twice the size of the lamb shoulder, overlapping on a countertop and put several spoonfuls of the paste in the center. Put the shoulder onto the plastic wrap, rib-bone side up, and then pour any remaining paste over the shoulder. Wrap the plastic around the shoulder. Repeat with a second layer of plastic around the shoulder to avoid any leaking. Put the shoulder into a baking dish and refrigerate overnight.

Preheat the oven to 250°F (120°C).

Unwrap the lamb shoulder and put it and any of the paste into a roasting pan. Cover with a sheet of parchment paper and then foil. Put the shoulder into the oven and roast for 6 hours. Remove the pan from the oven and let the meat rest for 30 minutes.

Transfer the lamb shoulder to a cutting board and carve it. Serve with the smoked raisin relish.

SMOKED RAISIN RELISH

3 cups (10.6 ounces) / 300 grams **large red raisins**

2 cups / 450 grams **white grape juice**

1½ tablespoons / 25 grams **honey**

3½ tablespoons / 50 grams **rice vinegar**

½ teaspoon / 3 grams **fine sea salt**

LAMB SHOULDER

9 tablespoons plus 1 teaspoon packed / 125 grams **light brown sugar**

⅓ cup / 75 grams **red wine**

3 tablespoons plus 2 teaspoons / 60 grams **tamari soy sauce**

5 tablespoons plus 2 teaspoons / 35 grams **smoked paprika**

2½ tablespoons / 15 grams **ground cumin**

2½ teaspoons / 14.5 grams **fine sea salt**

6 pounds 6 ounces / 2.9 kilograms **lamb shoulder**

WE HIGHLY RECOMMEND GRINDING YOUR OWN MEAT FOR
burgers, as the flavor and freshness of the meat is like nothing you can buy in a store. Butter may seem like an odd choice for a burger, but let's think about this: Butter comes from milk, which comes from cows, and so you're adding beef fat to your burger, just from a different source. We add onions to the mixture as well, grinding them with the meat, and as the burger cooks, the flavor of the onions permeates the meat, giving it an incredible savory flavor. We sear the burgers in a cast-iron skillet, which creates a crusty exterior that gives way to soft juicy meat inside. Contrary to popular belief, burgers cook more quickly and evenly if you flip them regularly, as long as you don't press down on the meat as it cooks. Try cooking them this way and see if you don't end up with a better burger. These are big messy burgers and that's just the way we like them.

2 pounds 6 ounces / 1.1 kilograms **boneless first-cut beef chuck roast**

⅔ cup / 200 grams chopped **onion**

14 tablespoons / 200 grams **unsalted butter,** diced

3 tablespoons / 50 grams **tamari soy sauce**

1¾ teaspoons / 10.5 grams **fine sea salt,** plus more for the skillet

¼ teaspoon / 0.5 gram **cayenne pepper**

MAKES 8 BURGERS

BUTTER BURGER

Cut the trimmed meat into strips that will fit into a meat grinder. Put the strips into a bowl sitting over ice to keep cold.

To the bowl of meat, add the onion, butter, soy sauce, salt, and cayenne. Grind the mixture through a meat grinder with a ¼-inch (6 mm) die. Run half of the ground meat mixture through the grinder a second time, return to the bowl, and gently mix everything together. Lay two sheets of plastic wrap on a counter slightly overlapping so that a double-wide piece of plastic wrap is formed. Form the meat into a log down the center of the plastic wrap. Fold the plastic over the log, pulling and tucking it under the meat like a giant sushi roll. Once you've rolled the log up in the plastic wrap, tighten the ends. Holding on to the ends, roll the cylinder on the countertop to tighten the plastic around the meat, forming a perfect, tight cylinder. The roll should be the width of a burger patty, which should be slightly larger than the diameter of your buns. We aim for 5 inches (13 cm) in diameter. Put the burger roll in the refrigerator to firm up, at least 1 hour and up to 12.

When you are ready to cook the burgers, slice the cylinder into 8 equal pieces, cutting through the plastic wrap. Unwrap the burgers. Set a large cast-iron skillet (you may want to use 2 pans at once) over medium-high heat and sprinkle a fine layer of salt on the bottom of the pan. Once the pan is hot, put 3 or 4 burgers in it and cook for 2 to 3 minutes. They will begin to render some of their fat into the pan and set on the bottom. Flip the burgers and cook the other side for 2 to 3 minutes. Continue to flip the burgers every minute or so until they are cooked the way you like them, 6 to 8 minutes total for medium-rare.

FIRST GRIND

SECOND GRIND

THIS IS A PLAY ON SURF AND TURF. SEAWEED IS RICH IN minerals and umami flavor and makes for a wonderful briny contrast to beef. There are a surprising variety of seaweeds available, most of which are sold dried, and each of which has its own distinct flavor and texture. Here we've taken a blend of dried seaweeds, hydrated them in a flavorful liquid, and pureed them with garlic, anchovies, and fresh parsley into an original version of salsa verde. The sauce is not a bright vibrant green, but what it lacks in beauty it more than makes up for in flavor. Any leftover salsa verde is delicious with steamed vegetables and fish and as a sauce for pasta.

SERVES 4

GRILLED RIB EYES
WITH SEAWEED SALSA VERDE

MARINATE THE RIB EYES: In a small bowl, combine the dark brown sugar, salt, garlic powder, onion powder, and cayenne and stir to blend well. Lay the rib eyes on a cutting board and sprinkle liberally with the salt mixture, patting it into the meat. Flip the meat over and generously season the other side. Put the meat on a wire rack set over a large plate or small baking sheet. Refrigerate uncovered for at least 2 hours and up to 24 hours.

MAKE THE SEAWEED SALSA VERDE: In a large bowl, combine the nori (tearing it up if necessary), dulse, kombu, garlic, anchovies and their oil, capers with their brine, lemon juice, vinegar, fish sauce, soy sauce, and sesame oil and let the seaweed hydrate in the liquids, about 10 minutes.

Bring a large pot of water to a boil over high heat. Cut the bottom ends of the parsley stems off. Blanch the parsley in the boiling water for 1 minute. Drain the parsley and put the hot parsley in a blender. Add the seaweed mixture and olive oil. Turn the blender on low and increase the speed to high, occasionally turning the blender off and scraping down the sides to make sure the mixture is completely pureed. When the salsa verde is completely smooth, turn the blender off and strain it through a fine-mesh sieve. It will be thick and a distinct drab olive color. Refrigerate

(recipe continues)

RIB EYES

2 tablespoons packed / 27 grams **dark brown sugar**

1 tablespoon / 18 grams **fine sea salt**

½ teaspoon / 1 gram **garlic powder**

½ teaspoon / 1 gram **onion powder**

Scant ¼ teaspoon / 0.5 gram **cayenne pepper**

2 (1½-pound / 750-gram) **rib eye steaks**

SEAWEED SALSA VERDE

3 sheets **nori**

0.9 ounce / 25 grams **dried dulse** or wakame

0.5 ounce / 15 grams **dried kombu**

5 medium **garlic** cloves

SEAWEED SALSA VERDE

the salsa verde in a covered container until ready to use. Leftover salsa verde will keep for up to 5 days.

Preheat a grill to high heat (500°F/260°C). Remove the rib eyes from the refrigerator and let them sit for 20 minutes to come to room temperature.

Put the meat on the grill and let it cook for 1 minute. Use a spatula to flip the meat onto a clean part of the grill. Cook the meat for 1 minute and then flip it again. Cook the meat for 30 seconds and flip it again. Continue to cook and flip the meat until it has cooked for 8 to 10 minutes total for medium-rare. The constant flipping promotes rapid, even cooking of the meat. Remove the meat to a large rimmed baking sheet or individual plates and cover with foil. Let the meat rest in a warm spot for 5 minutes.

Carve the meat into thick slices and serve with the seaweed salsa verde.

2.8 ounces / 80 grams **oil-packed anchovies (about 20)**

5 tablespoons plus 1 teaspoon / 40 grams **capers and their brine**

¼ cup plus 1 teaspoon / 60 grams **fresh lemon juice (from 2 lemons)**

2 tablespoons / 28 grams **rice vinegar**

4 teaspoons / 20 grams **fish sauce**

1½ teaspoons / 8 grams **tamari soy sauce**

1 teaspoon / 5 grams **sesame oil**

1 large bunch fresh **parsley**

¼ cup / 56 grams **olive oil**

CHATEAUBRIAND IS A LARGE PIECE OF CENTER-CUT FILET mignon that is meant for two people. In this recipe, we cured the meat with blue cheese to mimic the flavor effect of dry-aging. We keep a layer of cheesecloth between the meat and the blue cheese in order to make it easy to remove the cheese at the end of the curing time. The process gives the beef a wonderful flavor. You can use any blue cheese that you prefer. We like Gorgonzola dolce, but there's no need to make a special purchase if you normally keep a different kind on hand. A quick roast in a cast-iron skillet and a red wine pan sauce are all the meat needs post curing. You'll be amazed at how rich and intense this dish tastes.

1½ pounds / 780 grams
center-cut filet mignon

4 ounces / 113 grams
blue cheese, at room
temperature

2 tablespoons / 28 grams
olive oil

Fine sea salt

4 tablespoons / 56 grams
cold **unsalted butter,** diced

A few sprigs **fresh thyme**

½ cup / 115 grams good
red wine

SERVES 4

BLUE CHEESE–CURED CHATEAUBRIAND

Take a large piece of cheesecloth, dampen it with cool water, and wring it out. Wrap it around the meat and then smear the cheesecloth with the blue cheese so that the entire piece of meat is covered. Wrap the entire thing in plastic wrap and refrigerate it for 48 hours.

Preheat the oven to 425°F (220°C).

Unwrap the meat; carefully remove the cheesecloth and discard. Put the meat on a plate and set a large cast-iron or other heavy ovenproof skillet over medium heat. Add the olive oil to the pan, and once it begins to shimmer, season the meat with salt and put it in the pan. Sear the meat until the bottom is a deep golden brown, about 5 minutes, then flip the meat, and put the pan in the oven to finish cooking. For medium-rare, cook for 10 to 12 minutes or until the internal temperature reaches 120°–125°F (49°–52°C).

(recipe continues)

Take the pan out of the oven and add 2 tablespoons (28 grams) of the butter and the thyme sprigs. Baste the meat constantly until the butter has stopped foaming. Transfer the meat to a cutting board and cover loosely with foil and a kitchen towel to keep warm.

Pour the oil and herbs out of the pan, discard them, and set the pan over medium-low heat. Pour in the red wine and stir with a silicone spatula, scraping up any browned bits stuck to the bottom. Bring the wine to a simmer, reduce the heat to low, and add the remaining 2 tablespoons (28 grams) butter. Swirl the butter into the wine until the butter is absorbed and the sauce thickens and turns glossy. Immediately pour the sauce into a serving bowl.

Slice the chateaubriand and serve immediately with the sauce alongside.

> We love the technique of wrapping proteins in cheesecloth, applying a strong seasoning to the outside of the cheesecloth, and then wrapping and refrigerating to let the flavors transfer. It works beautifully and the layer of cheesecloth protects the ingredient inside, making it easy to remove the cure when it's ready. We've used it with meat, fish, and vegetables with miso, cheese, herb purees, and wet spice mixtures for the outer seasoning layer.

WRAPPED AND SMOTHERED IN
BLUE CHEESE; UNWRAPPED,
AFTER CURING

MOST PEOPLE THINK TO BRAISE SHORT RIBS, BUT ROASTING them is much easier and really emphasizes the deep meaty flavor of this cut. Slow-roasting allows the outside of the rib to caramelize while the meat slowly becomes tender and the fat renders, becoming like the outside edge of a great well-seasoned roast of beef: crispy, chewy, tender, and rich. It's a messy dish meant to be eaten with fingers and whatever other utensils are deemed necessary and happily accompanied by a great red wine.

SERVES 6 TO 8

ROASTED
SHORT RIBS

8 meaty **bone-in beef short ribs** (about 4 pounds / 1.8 kilograms total)

4 teaspoons / 24 grams **fine sea salt**

3 tablespoons packed / 40 grams **light brown sugar**

2 teaspoons / 4 grams **smoked paprika**

Use a knife to remove any silver skin and surface fat from the short ribs. In a small bowl, stir together the salt, brown sugar, and smoked paprika. Season the ribs all over with the seasoning mixture, rubbing it into the meat. Put the ribs on a wire rack on a baking sheet and refrigerate uncovered overnight.

Preheat the oven to 250°F (120°C).

Transfer the baking sheet to the oven and roast for 3 hours 30 minutes, basting occasionally, until tender and caramelized. Remove from the oven and let rest for 10 minutes before serving.

RIBS SPRINKLED WITH SEASONING

YOU MAY WONDER WHY ANYONE WOULD GO TO THE TROUBLE TO cook steak sous vide at home. The simplest answer is that it's the best way to ensure a perfectly cooked, flavorful interior and a nicely charred exterior; in other words, you'll never overcook an expensive cut of meat again (see page 180). To add richness and depth of flavor to the finished steak, we caramelize the fat layer on the outside of the porterhouse before cooking the steak sous vide. The sauce uses caramelized brown butter solids to further enhance the beefy flavor of the meal.

One important tip to make this method foolproof: Do not salt the meat before you cook it in the water bath. Salt pulls all of the juice out of the meat as it cooks, which leaves you with perfectly pink, bone dry meat. Saving the salt for the final cooking period ensures that after cooking sous vide you will have juicy, flavorful meat, ready for the grill—which is the right time to season.

Pair with Tomato and Nori Salad (page 90) or the Lemon Roasted Potatoes (page 125) for a great summertime meal.

12 ounces / 345 grams **unsalted butter**

¾ cup / 120 grams **nonfat dry milk**

¾ cup / 195 grams **ketchup**

¾ cup / 180 grams **prepared horseradish**

⅔ cup / 155 grams **brewed coffee**

1 (2¼-pound / 1-kilogram) **porterhouse steak**, 2- to 2½ inches / about 5 cm thick

¾ teaspoon / 4.5 grams **fine sea salt**

Fleur de sel, for serving (optional)

SERVES 2

SLOW-COOKED PORTERHOUSE

In a medium saucepan, melt the butter over low heat. Add the dry milk powder and stir to combine. Cook, stirring constantly, until the solids turn a rich caramel color, 10 to 15 minutes. Remove the pan from the heat and let cool.

Strain the mixture through a fine-mesh sieve. Reserve the butter. Put the milk solids into a blender with the ketchup, horseradish, and coffee. Turn the blender on low, then increase the speed to high, and puree for 1 to 2 minutes until it is smooth. Strain the brown butter steak sauce through a fine-mesh sieve and reserve in the refrigerator.

(recipe continues)

Heat a large cast-iron skillet over medium-high heat. Use a paring knife to score the fat on the long side of the porterhouse in a crosshatch pattern. When the pan is hot, hold the porterhouse fat edge down in the pan to sear and render the fat, 2 to 3 minutes. Reduce the heat to medium and continue to caramelize the fat for 2 more minutes until it is completely golden brown. Remove the steak from the pan and transfer it to a wire rack set over a baking sheet and refrigerate it to cool.

Preheat a circulating water bath or large pot of water to 131°F (55°C); see page 180.

Put the steak into a vacuum bag with 4 tablespoons (56 grams) of the reserved butter, saving the rest for another use, and seal. Alternatively, put the steak and butter into a zip-top bag, remove the air, and seal. Cook in the water bath for 3 hours. You can finish the steak on the grill immediately or transfer to an ice water bath to cool the meat down, about 30 minutes. The chilled steak may be kept in the refrigerator for up to 48 hours before grilling.

To reheat the steak, preheat a circulating water bath or large pot of water to 131°F (55°C); see page 180.

Put the steak, still in its bag, in the water bath and let it cook for 10 minutes to warm the steak through. Open the bag and put the steak on a large plate, discarding the butter, pat it dry, and season with the salt.

To finish cooking, preheat a grill so that it is extremely hot, at least 500°F (260°C).

Grill the steak, flipping it every 30 seconds, until the exterior is evenly marked and deeply caramelized, about 3 minutes. Transfer the meat to a platter to rest for at least 5 minutes. Put the meat on a large cutting board. Use a knife to remove the filet and strip loin from the bone. Slice the meat into ½-inch (13 mm) slices and rearrange the meat around the bone on the platter. Serve immediately with fleur de sel, and the brown butter steak sauce.

SLOW-COOKED HANGER STEAK

ANOTHER WONDERFUL THING ABOUT SOUS VIDE COOKING is that you can take a less expensive steak, like hanger, one of our favorite cuts, and turn it into a dish as special and delicious as a pricey porterhouse. Also known as the hanging tender or the butcher's steak, hanger steak is characterized by its slightly gamey flavor due to its position inside the rib cage near several internal organs. It is usually butchered into two slightly irregular, long steaks because there is a layer of connective tissue that runs through the center of the meat. Combining two methods—slow-cooking at a low temperature to soften and gelatinize the connective tissue and then grilling to sear the outside and add a smoky flavor—results in a truly superior steak that's pink throughout and has a surprisingly deep, juicy flavor. Note that you may need to special order the whole hanger steaks from your butcher; hanger steaks often come butchered in two to remove that connective tissue, which, in this recipe, softens and becomes deliciously edible, eliminating waste.

Follow the recipe for Slow-Cooked Porterhouse, substituting two 2¼-pound (1-kilogram) **whole hanger steaks** and making the following alterations: Skip the pan-searing step. Cook the hanger steaks in the water bath for 24 hours instead of 3. When seasoning with salt before grilling, increase the amount to 1¾ teaspoons (10.5 grams) **fine sea salt.** Grill for about 6 minutes, flipping the meat every 30 seconds or so. Let it rest for 5 to 10 minutes. Slice each hanger steak crosswise into ¾-inch (2 cm) slices.

SLOW-COOKED WHOLE HANGAR STEAK; THE CONNECTIVE TISSUE HAS BEEN CONVERTED INTO SUCCULENT GELATIN AND IS COMPLETELY EDIBLE.

SOUS VIDE & CONTROLLED-TEMPERATURE COOKING

In French, the term *sous vide* means "under vacuum." In modern cooking terms, this definition has morphed to apply to foods cooked in a water bath at controlled temperatures. While the foods in question are often vacuum-sealed, the term is more about the style of cooking than about the fact that you may use a vacuum sealer. In fact, you don't need a vacuum sealer to use a controlled-temperature water bath. You can use heavy-duty zip-top bags designed for the freezer; just be sure to remove all of the air from the bag so that your food doesn't float.

Sous vide equipment in the form of immersion circulators, which heat and circulate water, is becoming less expensive, and there are several home versions on the market. That said, understandably many people want to test out the technique before spending up to $500 for equipment. The easiest way to make your own controlled-temperature water bath at home is to use a large (16-quart/16-liter) stockpot and a thermometer, preferably a probe with a sensor that sits in the water and is connected to a digital readout that sits on your counter. The size of the pot is important because if it is too small it will

get too hot even at the lowest burner setting. Fill the stockpot about three-quarters of the way to the top and set it over low heat until it reaches the desired temperature. Keep an eye on the temperature, stirring the water every so often, increasing or lowering the heat until you figure out the right level to maintain the temperature in your water bath.

If you don't have a vacuum sealer, seal the food in zip-top bags; you can clip the tops to the top of the stockpot for extra security. Once you add the food you will have to adjust the heat again to find the level you need to maintain the desired temperature. Once you've reached a pretty stable temperature, you will only have to check it periodically to make sure it's holding steady and make any adjustments necessary. Then proceed with the recipe.

We have a limited number of sous vide recipes in this book. The ones we included showcase why the technique is important. It is a wonderfully efficient cooking method that helps get the most out of ingredients; for example, the hanger steak is almost never seen as a whole roast but using the circulator allows to you to gelatinize the connective tissue that runs through the center of the meat, which adds a wonderful beefy flavor and tender texture to the steak. You can then caramelize the exterior and the entire cut of meat becomes edible and delicious, with no waste. The use of sous vide elevates a second-tier cut into something truly special. Another thing we love about this technique is that we can infuse flavor into the ingredients during the first step by sealing them in a bag with various aromatics. Then we add another layer of flavor with our final seasoning and by searing the food before serving.

We've found that steaming is a wonderful alternative to sous vide cookery and is accessible to everyone at home. While you don't have the ability to adjust your temperatures in the same way, the fact that you can maintain a specific temperature using moist heat makes it extremely useful for a variety of preparations. There are significantly more steaming recipes in the book because they are so efficient. In many cases it takes the place of blanching in our kitchen because it is easier to control and does a much better job of preserving the flavor of ingredients.

We also like the technique of pressure steaming: We put water in the bottom of a pressure cooker, add a rack, and then put the ingredients in a smaller, open container (usually a stainless steel bowl) that fits on the rack inside. You get even steaming at slightly higher temperatures than a traditional steamer and at uniform pressure for rapid, even cooking. It's like steaming on steroids.

Science says that foods do not absorb flavor from the steaming liquid, but our experiments in the pressure cooker have proven that this is not the case at all. Lemon zest, herbs, sliced ginger, and other aromatics will permeate the ingredients steamed over them. It's an easy way to add flavor to your food. The moist heat is wonderful because it hydrates your ingredients as they cook. We love steamed buns, and you can turn almost any bread dough into a soft, pillowy end product if you steam instead of bake. Pressure-steamed potatoes make fabulous French fries (page 123), and the technique allows you to parcook them in advance. We also find that the results tend to be fluffier and we avoid the pitfall of the empty French fry where all the potato filling somehow disappears into the crust.

INSPIRED BY MANY PEOPLE'S FAVORITE PIZZA, THIS LASAGNA has a meat sauce studded with pepperoni, which adds a savory depth of flavor. This is a big recipe, enough for two dinners or one big party. Lasagna is one of those dishes that keeps well and is a little bit of work to prepare. Making two is almost as easy as making one, and then you have an extra stashed in the freezer for a rainy day. We use the pressure cooker to make the sauce, so there are no long hours spent stirring a pot at the back of the stove. Once you have the sauce, everything comes together fairly easily. Then you can stick the casserole in the oven and enjoy cocktails with your guests until the timer goes off and dinner is ready to be served.

**MAKES 2 LASAGNAS/
SERVES 16**

PEPPERONI LASAGNA

In a large bowl, combine the celery, onion, carrots, and ½ pound (225 grams) of the pepperoni. Stir well. Transfer half of the mixture to a food processor, and pulse to evenly mince. Transfer to a pressure cooker and repeat with the remaining mixture.

Add the beef, veal, pork, white wine, canned tomatoes, fish sauce, and 1 teaspoon (6 grams) of the salt to the pressure cooker. Use a rubber spatula to stir the mixture together and then cook at high pressure for 30 minutes. Let the pressure dissipate naturally and let the sauce cool in a bowl set over an ice water bath.

Preheat the oven to 325°F (165°C).

Set a medium pot of water and a large pot of salted water over high heat and bring them to a boil. When the medium pot of water reaches a boil, blanch the basil leaves and stems for 1 minute and transfer to an ice water bath. Squeeze the basil dry and put it into a blender with the ricotta, nutmeg, and remaining ½ teaspoon (3 grams) salt. Turn the blender on low and increase the speed to high. Puree the mixture until it is light green and smooth. Turn the blender off and strain the mixture through a fine-mesh sieve. Reserve the basil ricotta in the refrigerator.

3 **celery** ribs, cut into 1-inch / 2.5 cm pieces

1 large **onion,** cut into 1-inch / 2.5 cm pieces

5 medium **carrots,** cut into 1-inch / 2.5 cm pieces

1¼ pounds / 565 grams thinly sliced **pepperoni**

1 pound / 450 grams **ground beef**

1 pound / 450 grams **ground veal**

1 pound / 450 grams **ground pork**

1 cup / 225 grams **dry white wine**

1 (28-ounce / 800-gram) can **whole tomatoes**

2 tablespoons / 28 grams **fish sauce**

1½ teaspoons / 9 grams **fine sea salt**

2 small bunches / 42 grams fresh **basil**

3 cups / 735 grams fresh **ricotta cheese,** homemade (page 54) or store-bought

½ teaspoon / 1 gram freshly grated **nutmeg**

2 pounds / 900 grams **lasagna noodles**

1½ pounds / 680 grams sliced **provolone cheese**

2 pounds / 900 grams **fresh mozzarella cheese**

Put one-quarter of the pepperoni sauce into a large bowl, and put another one-quarter of the sauce in another large bowl. Put 1 pound (450 grams) of the lasagna noodles into the large pot of boiling water and cook until they are just flexible but not cooked through, about 5 minutes. Use a slotted spoon to remove the noodles from the water and put them into the first bowl with sauce. Use a spoon to evenly coat the noodles with the cold sauce. Repeat with the second box of noodles and the second bowl of sauce. Line the bottom of one 9 × 13-inch (23 × 33 cm) baking pan with an even layer of pepperoni slices. Top the pepperoni with a layer of sauced noodles. Spoon one-quarter of the basil ricotta over the noodles and top with one-quarter of the provolone. Put a second layer of noodles into the pan and top them with half of the remaining sauce. Put one-quarter of the basil ricotta on top of the noodles. Arrange a second layer of pepperoni over the ricotta and a second layer of provolone on top of the pepperoni. Arrange the last of the first bowl of noodles on top and spoon the remaining sauce from the bowl over them. Put a final layer of pepperoni over the noodles and then tear 1 pound (450 grams) of the mozzarella into bite-size pieces and top the lasagna. Repeat with the remaining ingredients and a second pan to make another lasagna and refrigerate or cover and freeze for another time. The lasagna will keep in the refrigerator for 5 days and in the freezer for a month.

Put the lasagna on a baking sheet and bake, uncovered, for 1 hour 30 minutes. The cheese should be lightly browned and the lasagna should be bubbling. Turn the oven off and let the lasagna rest in the oven for 15 minutes. Remove the lasagna from the oven and serve.

CAKES

THIS CAKE IS A MARRIAGE BETWEEN ENGLISH STICKY TOFFEE
pudding and American carrot cake. It manages to have rich
texture and be incredibly light at the same time. It cooks in half
of its sauce in the manner of classic pudding cakes and then
the remainder is served alongside, hence the sticky part of the
title. We add creamy coconut flavor to balance the sweetness of
the carrot. The two work beautifully together to give the finished
cake a haunting flavor. Coconut nectar, a relatively new product
that's found in most health food stores or at Whole Foods, is
a natural sweetener made from the sap of coconut trees. You
can easily substitute cane syrup. Either juice your own carrots
and ginger or head over to the nearest juice bar and pick some
up. They add great depth of flavor to the finished cake. Don't
be daunted by the long ingredients list, as everything comes
together quite easily. Eaten warm with Banana Caramel Ice
Cream (page 243), this cake is simply transcendent. Serve it
after a lighter meal because everyone will definitely want to have
room for dessert.

SERVES 8

COCONUT SAUCE

2 cups / 512 grams **coconut milk**

6 tablespoons plus 2 teaspoons packed / 90 grams **light brown sugar**

3 tablespoons plus 2 teaspoons / 55 grams **coconut nectar**

½ teaspoon / 3 grams **fine sea salt**

½ teaspoon / 2 grams **vanilla extract**

STICKY
CARROT COCONUT
PUDDING

Preheat the oven to 350°F (175°C). Butter an 8-inch (20 cm) square baking
dish that's at least 3 inches (8 cm) deep.

MAKE THE COCONUT SAUCE: In a medium saucepan, combine the
coconut milk, brown sugar, coconut nectar, and salt. Bring the mixture
to a boil over medium-high heat, stirring often to melt the sugar. Reduce
the heat and simmer, stirring constantly, for about 5 minutes. Stir in
the vanilla. Pour half of the sauce into the prepared baking dish and put
the dish in the refrigerator. Let the remaining sauce cool and reserve in a
covered container in the refrigerator until you're ready to serve the cake.

MAKE THE CAKE: In a medium saucepan, combine the dates, carrot juice, ginger juice, allspice, cinnamon, nutmeg, and cloves and set over medium-high heat. Once the mixture begins to boil, remove the pan from the heat and stir in the baking soda. Put the mixture in a blender and puree on low. Increase the speed to medium high and puree until smooth. Scrape the mixture into a bowl. Set aside at room temperature.

In a stand mixer fitted with the paddle attachment, beat the butter, granulated sugar, baking powder, and salt until light and fluffy. Gradually beat in the eggs and vanilla on medium-low speed. Don't worry if the mixture looks a bit curdled. Add half of the flour, mixing on low until it is incorporated, and then add all of the date mixture, mixing on low until it is absorbed. Add all of the remaining flour and mix on low until it is just blended. Don't overbeat the batter.

Remove the baking dish from the refrigerator and scrape the batter into the dish. Bake until the cake is just firm and a cake tester inserted in the center comes out with moist crumbs attached, 40 to 45 minutes. Remove the pan from the oven and let the cake cool slightly before serving. Serve warm with the reserved coconut sauce.

DATES (the fruit of date palm tree) are drupes, characterized by the fact that the flesh surrounds the seed. Usually found in the dried fruit section of supermarkets, they are intensely sweet and rich in flavor with a relatively thick skin and tender flesh. They are good sources of fiber, and contain tannins, vitamins, calcium, magnesium, and iron. They are delicious eaten out of hand; when added to baked goods, like Sticky Carrot Coconut Pudding, they add moisture and a complex sweetness that will leave your taste buds begging for more.

CAKE

6 ounces / 180 grams **pitted dates,** chopped

1 cup / 225 grams **carrot juice**

¼ cup / 56 grams **ginger juice**

½ teaspoon / 1 gram **ground allspice**

½ teaspoon / 1 gram **ground cinnamon**

½ teaspoon / 1 gram **freshly grated nutmeg**

¼ teaspoon / 0.5 gram **ground cloves**

1 teaspoon / 5 grams **baking soda**

4 tablespoon / 56 grams **unsalted butter**

¾ cup / 150 grams **granulated sugar**

1 teaspoon / 6 grams **baking powder**

½ teaspoon / 3 grams **fine sea salt**

2 large **eggs,** at room temperature

1 teaspoon / 4 grams **vanilla extract**

1 cup plus 2½ tablespoons / 175 grams **all-purpose flour**

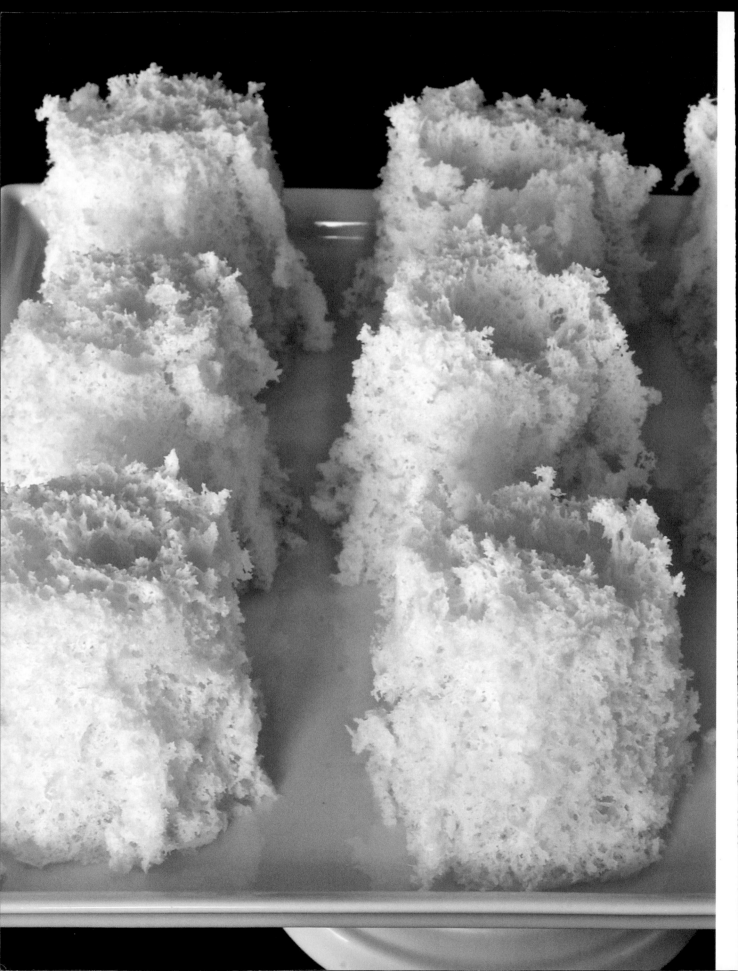

ALBERT ADRIÀ DEVELOPED THE ORIGINAL MICROWAVE SPONGE cake at the iconic Spanish restaurant El Bulli: The N_2O from a whipped cream dispenser acts as the leavening, and the microwave provides a uniform cooking environment that helps create the finished texture of the cake. We loved the idea of his little creations and wanted to play around with different flavors in our own kitchen. The first time we made these lemon cakes, the only paper cups in the house were printed with Tinker Bell and her fairies. Once we tasted the cakes, we realized that fairy cakes was the perfect description for these dainty morsels filled with bright lemon flavor that almost seem to dissolve on your tongue. The tangy citrus paired with the subtle heat from the cayenne wakes up your palate and leaves you automatically reaching for more.

MAKES 12 CAKES

MICROWAVE LEMON FAIRY CAKES

MAKE THE MICROWAVE LEMON CURD: Put the butter in a small microwave-safe bowl and microwave on high for 45 seconds until the butter is melted but not hot. In a large microwave-safe bowl, whisk together the lemon juice, whole eggs, sugar, salt, and cayenne until smooth. Stir in the melted butter. Put the bowl in the microwave and cook for 1 minute on high power. Remove the bowl from the microwave and stir with a spatula. There may not be any visible change yet. Microwave for 1 minute more. Remove from the microwave and stir. The mixture will appear hot but will still look basically the same. Microwave on high for 1 minute more. Remove the bowl from the microwave—at this point the mixture will have thickened on the sides. Stir and then microwave for 1 minute more, for a total of 4 minutes. Remove the bowl from the microwave. At first glance the mixture will look semi-scrambled. Stir and it will become smooth, shiny, and thick. Put the bowl of lemon curd in an ice water bath. When the lemon curd has chilled, use it immediately or refrigerate it in a covered container for up to 3 days.

(recipe continues)

MICROWAVE LEMON CURD

4 tablespoons / 56 grams **unsalted butter**

½ cup plus 2 tablespoons / 140 grams **fresh lemon juice** (from 4 lemons)

4 large **eggs**

1 cup / 200 grams **sugar**

½ teaspoon / 3 grams **fine sea salt**

⅛ teaspoon / 0.25 gram **cayenne pepper**

CHILLING THE LEMON CURD

MAKE THE FAIRY CAKES: Put the lemon curd and egg whites in a blender. Turn the blender on to low and increase the speed to medium-high. When the mixture is loose, sprinkle in the egg white powder and flour. Puree the mixture for 30 seconds until the egg white powder and flour are fully absorbed and the mixture is smooth.

Transfer the batter into the 1-liter canister of an iSi whipped cream dispenser and put the lid on. Charge with one N_2O charger and then shake to distribute the gas and allow it to be absorbed into the batter. Repeat with a second charger. The batter should feel and sound fluid in the canister. The batter may be used immediately or stored in the canister in the refrigerator for up to 24 hours. Shake vigorously before using.

Prepare twelve 10-ounce paper cups by turning them over and using a paring knife to make a small slit in the bottom of each cup and 3 small slits around the sides to let steam vent as the cakes cook. Turn the cups right side up and set them on the counter. Shake the whipped cream canister and dispense batter into a cup, filling it one-third of the way up. Put the cup into the microwave and cook on high for 30 seconds. Immediately remove it from the microwave and invert the cup (with the cake still in it) onto a cutting board or countertop. Let the cake cool in this position while cooking the remaining cakes. Repeat the process of filling the cups and cooking the cakes until you've used all 12 cups. Let the lemon cakes cool until the cups are no longer hot to the touch.

To serve, run a paring knife around the inside of the cups to loosen the cakes. Gently shake each cup to remove the cake; they will have a honeycombed appearance like small sponges. Alternatively, the cakes may be stored in the cups, inverted in the refrigerator, overnight.

FAIRY CAKES

2 large **egg whites**

5 tablespoons plus
2 teaspoons / 24 grams
egg white powder

½ cup / 75 grams
all-purpose flour

CARAMEL CAKE IS A CLASSIC SOUTHERN CAKE THAT OFTEN
sounds better than it actually tastes. Part of the issue is that
caramel is so sweet that you need to find a way to balance it in
order to truly enjoy the flavor; oftentimes the combination of
sweet cake and sweet glaze is just too much. We came up with
the idea of using a bit of extra lactic acid—the acid found in dairy
products—in the form of buttermilk powder in the cake batter
to make it sharp enough to stand up to the caramel glaze. A bit
of strawberry jam between the layers adds a different kind of
acidity and brightness, leaving you with a cake that disappears
almost as quickly as you can cut it. If you happen to be the kind
of person who prefers frosting to a glaze, you can simply beat
1½ cups (170 grams) confectioners' sugar into the lukewarm
glaze and it will make a super-creamy frosting instead.

MAKES ONE 8-INCH / 20 CM
LAYER CAKE

CARAMEL CAKE

MAKE THE CAKE: Preheat the oven to 350°F (175°C). Butter and flour two
8-inch (20 cm) round cake pans.

In a stand mixer fitted with the paddle attachment, beat the butter,
sugar, buttermilk powder, baking powder, and salt until light and fluffy.
With the mixer running on medium-low, add the eggs one at a time,
mixing until each egg is fully absorbed before adding the next.

In a small bowl, stir together the buttermilk and vanilla. Add one-
third of the flour to the mixer, and when it is almost absorbed, add half
of the buttermilk mixture. When the buttermilk is almost absorbed, add
the next third of the flour, followed by the remaining buttermilk mixture
and last third of flour. Divide the batter evenly between the prepared cake
pans and rap them on the counter a few times to release any air bubbles.

Bake until the cakes are just firm to the touch or the internal
temperature registers 190–195°F (87–90°C), 20 to 25 minutes. Let them
cool in the pans for 10 minutes and then turn them out onto a wire rack
to cool completely.

(recipe continues)

CAKE

8 ounces / 225 grams
unsalted butter, at room
temperature

1¾ cups / 350 grams **sugar**

1 tablespoon / 9 grams
buttermilk powder

1 tablespoon / 18 grams
baking powder

1 teaspoon / 6 grams **fine
sea salt**

4 large **eggs,** at room
temperature

1¼ cups / 300 grams
cultured buttermilk,
homemade (page 54) or
store-bought, at room
temperature

1 teaspoon / 4 grams **vanilla
extract**

3 cups / 450 grams
all-purpose flour

Once the cake layers are cool, use a large serrated knife to trim one of the tops so that it is perfectly flat. Save the cake trimmings so that you can dehydrate them and use them for other recipes (see page 37). (You can wrap the cake layers in plastic wrap and refrigerate them for up to 24 hours before finishing the cake.) Cut each layer in half, creating four layers.

MEANWHILE, MAKE THE CARAMEL GLAZE: In a deep, medium saucepan, combine the brown sugar, salt, and cream and set over medium heat, stirring to dissolve the sugar and salt. Cook the mixture, without stirring, until it reaches 240°F (116°C) on a candy thermometer. Remove the pan from the heat and stir in the butter; this will cause the caramel to bubble up. Once the caramel has stopped bubbling, stir it until smooth, then let it cool. Once the caramel has cooled to where it is thick but still liquid, you can use it to glaze the cake.

Set one layer, trimmed side up, on a rack set over a baking sheet. Use a small offset spatula to spread the strawberry jam evenly over the top. Repeat with two more layers. Cover with the final layer, top side up, so that there is a smooth surface on which to pour the caramel. Slowly pour the warm glaze over the cake, allowing it to run down the sides. Sprinkle the top with fleur de sel. Leave the cake alone for at least 30 minutes to allow the glaze to set before attempting to move the cake. Transfer to a platter and serve.

CARAMEL GLAZE

2¼ cups packed / 450 grams **light brown sugar**

½ teaspoon / 3 grams **fine sea salt**

1 cup / 240 grams **heavy cream**

2 tablespoons / 28 grams **unsalted butter**

¼ cup / 85 grams **Strawberry Jam** (recipe follows) or store-bought jelly

Fleur de sel

STRAWBERRY JAM

MAKES A SCANT QUART / LITER

2 pounds / 910 grams hulled **strawberries,** quartered

2 cups / 400 grams **sugar**

7 tablespoons / 100 grams **fresh lime juice** (from about 3½ limes)

¾ teaspoon / 4.5 grams **fine sea salt**

In a large saucepan, combine the strawberries, sugar, lime juice, and salt and set over medium heat, stirring to dissolve the sugar. Continue to cook, without stirring, until it reaches 219°F (104°C) and then transfer to a heatproof container to cool. The jam will keep for up to a month in the refrigerator.

THIS IS AN EASY CAKE THAT'S PERFECT TO HAVE IN YOUR BACK
pocket: It comes together quickly from pantry (and freezer) ingredients and can be eaten warm, straight from the oven. You can easily swap out ingredients, substituting blueberries and walnuts, peaches and pistachios, or pineapples and toasted coconut, for example. Since the cake is not overly sweet, the only caveat is that one of the mix-ins (usually the fruit) must be sweet enough to make it a real dessert. We use our heartier Batch 2 gluten-free flour here, but you can easily substitute What IiF Gluten-Free Flour (page 25), all-purpose, or even white whole wheat. It's a truly versatile cake that is always delicious.

MAKES ONE 9-INCH / 23 CM CAKE

1 cup / 113 grams **cherries,** pitted, fresh or thawed frozen

1 cup / 113 grams **pecan halves,** roasted (see page 39)

4 tablespoons / 56 grams **unsalted butter**

2 large **eggs**

½ cup / 100 grams **sugar**

½ teaspoon / 2 grams **vanilla extract**

¼ teaspoon / 1.5 grams **fine sea salt**

1 cup / 150 grams **Batch 2 Gluten-Free Flour** (page 25)

GLUTEN-FREE CHERRY PECAN CAKE

Preheat the oven to 350°F (175°C). Butter a 9-inch (23 cm) round cake pan.

Scatter the cherries and pecans in the bottom of the prepared pan. In a small saucepan, melt the butter over medium heat. Continue to cook it, swirling the pan, until the butter browns and gives off a nutty aroma, another 30 to 60 seconds. Remove the pan from the heat and cool slightly.

In a medium bowl, whisk together the eggs and sugar. While whisking constantly, slowly drizzle the brown butter into the egg mixture and whisk to blend. Add the vanilla and salt and whisk to blend. Add the flour and use a rubber spatula to stir it into the batter. Mix until the batter is smooth and shiny with a fluid texture. When you lift the spatula, the batter should fall back into the bowl in a ribbon. Pour the batter over the cherries and pecans.

Bake until the top is golden brown and the cake is just firm when pressed with your fingers, about 40 minutes. Let cool for 10 minutes in the pan and then turn it out onto a wire rack to cool. The cake may be served warm or at room temperature.

DURING COLD WINTER MONTHS, WHEN FRESH FRUITS ARE HARD
to come by, jams and jellies can be used to add flavor to cake
batters. This incredibly moist, decadent cake has swirls of
orange marmalade in the batter, making the layers beautiful
and delicious. It then gets drenched in orange juice–bourbon
syrup and finished off with bourbon buttercream. If orange isn't
your favorite flavor, you can easily substitute your favorite jelly
and corresponding juice. Cherry makes for a pretty wonderful
riff off this cake. Also, you can easily eliminate the bourbon to
make the cake kid-friendly, but we like to have a few surprisingly
sophisticated treats in our repertoire to pamper the adults in
our life.

**MAKES ONE 9-INCH / 23 CM
LAYER CAKE**

ORANGE
MARMALADE CAKE

MAKE THE CAKE: Position a rack in the middle of the oven and preheat it
to 350°F (175°C). Butter two 9-inch (23 cm) round cake pans and line the
bottoms with parchment paper.

In a stand mixer fitted with the paddle attachment, beat the butter,
sugar, baking powder, salt, ginger, and cinnamon on low speed until light
and fluffy. Stop the mixer and add all of the flour. Mix on low until just
blended.

In a medium bowl, whisk together the eggs, buttermilk, orange oil,
and blood orange bitters (if using) until well blended and slightly frothy.
With the mixer running on low speed, slowly drizzle the buttermilk
mixture into the mixer and then mix until the batter is smooth and
shiny. Stir the orange marmalade briefly to loosen it up and then use
a rubber spatula to gently fold it into the batter, using 4 to 6 strokes,
leaving streaks of marmalade running through it. Divide the batter evenly
between the prepared cake pans and rap the pans firmly on the counter a
few times to release any air bubbles.

(recipe continues)

CAKE

8 ounces / 225 grams
unsalted butter

1½ cups / 300 grams **sugar**

1 tablespoon / 18 grams
baking powder

1 teaspoon / 6 grams **fine
sea salt**

½ teaspoon / 1 gram **ground
ginger**

¼ teaspoon / 0.5 gram
ground cinnamon

3 cups / 450 grams
all-purpose flour

4 large **eggs**

1¼ cups / 300 grams
cultured buttermilk,
homemade (page 54) or
store-bought

¼ teaspoon / 1 gram
Boyajian orange oil, orange
extract, or orange essential
oil

½ teaspoon / 2 grams **blood
orange bitters** (optional)

1 cup / 300 grams **orange
marmalade,** at room
temperature

Bake until the cakes feel firm when gently pressed in their centers and are just starting to pull back from the sides of the pan or reach an internal temperature of 190°–195°F (87°–90°C), 30 to 35 minutes. Remove the pans from the oven and let the cakes cool in the pans on a wire rack for 15 minutes.

MEANWHILE, MAKE THE ORANGE SYRUP: In a bowl, whisk together the orange juice, bourbon, and sugar until the sugar has completely dissolved. Use a cake skewer or toothpick to pierce the cake layers, still in their pans, all over the top, leaving about 1 inch (2.5 cm) between holes. Spoon the syrup over the tops of the cakes, evenly dividing it between the pans. (Alternatively, if you have a brine injector or a stainless-steel turkey baster with an injection needle, you can use it to inject the syrup into the cake layers at 2-inch intervals, being careful not to push the tip all the way to the bottom of the cake.) Let the cakes cool completely in their pans.

ONCE THE CAKES ARE COOL, MAKE THE BOURBON BUTTERCREAM: In a stand mixer fitted with the paddle attachment, mix 1 cup of the confectioners' sugar, the butter, and salt on low speed until the sugar is completely absorbed. Add 1 more cup confectioners' sugar and mix on low until it is absorbed. Repeat with the remaining 2 cups sugar, beating until the mixture is fairly thick. Add the bourbon and mix until it is fully absorbed. Add the milk 1 tablespoon at a time until the frosting has reached a spreadable consistency that is to your liking.

TO FROST THE CAKE: Invert one of the cooled layers onto a cake circle or serving platter. If necessary, use a large serrated knife to trim off the top of the cake so that it is flat. Use one-quarter of the frosting to cover the top of the layer, leaving a ¼-inch (6 mm) border around the circumference. Carefully invert the second layer onto a piece of parchment or wax paper. Put the second layer, top side up, over the bottom layer, being sure to line up the sides evenly. Use the remaining frosting to cover the top and sides of the cake. Chill for at least 30 minutes to let the frosting set up before serving,

ORANGE SYRUP

½ cup plus 2 tablespoons / 140 grams **fresh orange juice**

2 tablespoons / 30 grams good **bourbon,** preferably Knob Creek

¼ cup / 50 grams **sugar**

BOURBON BUTTERCREAM

4 cups / 450 grams **confectioners' sugar**

8 ounces / 225 grams **unsalted butter,** at room temperature

¼ teaspoon / 1.5 grams **fine sea salt**

2 tablespoons / 30 grams good **bourbon,** preferably Knob Creek

2 to 3 tablespoons / 30 to 45 grams **whole milk**

CHEESECAKE HAS BEEN ONE OF AKI'S FAVORITE DESSERTS SINCE she was a kid. The very best versions have a crisp cookie crust to contrast with a lush, creamy exterior. Unlike the dense New York City version with cream cheese and sour cream and a somewhat dry, lightly browned exterior, this one is lighter and creamier and emphasizes the fresh flavor of the cheese. To do this, we bake the crust first and then cook the assembled cheesecake at a much lower temperature for a longer time so the custard has time to set throughout the cake and there is no chance of curdling or breaking. The result is silky smooth and close to perfection.

MAKES ONE 9-INCH / 23 CM CAKE

RICOTTA CHEESECAKE

Nonstick cooking spray

8 ounces / 225 grams **Bordeaux-Style Cookies** (page 228)

8 tablespoons / 113 grams **unsalted butter,** melted

3 cups / 735 grams fresh **ricotta cheese,** homemade (page 54) or store-bought

3 cups / 720 grams **crème fraîche,** homemade (page 55) or store-bought

1½ cups / 300 grams **sugar**

1 teaspoon / 6 grams **fine sea salt**

3 large **eggs**

Preheat the oven to 350°F (175°C). Coat a 9-inch (23 cm) springform pan with cooking spray and wipe it out with a paper towel, leaving a thin film behind.

Put the cookies in a food processor and pulse to crush them into a fine crumb. Add the melted butter and pulse a few times until the mixture clumps together. Pour the cookie crumbs into the prepared pan and use the bottom of a ½-cup measure to help press them in a uniform layer along the bottom and about 1 inch (2.5 cm) up the sides of the pan. Put the pan in the refrigerator to chill while the oven heats.

Put the springform pan on a baking sheet lined with a silicone mat or parchment paper and bake until the crust is golden brown and just set, about 10 minutes. Remove the pan from the oven and let cool at room temperature.

Reduce the oven temperature to 250°F (120°C).

In a medium bowl, use a rubber spatula to mix together the ricotta, crème fraîche, sugar, and salt. Add the eggs to the ricotta mixture and mix with the rubber spatula to blend everything together until smooth. Pour into the cooled cake pan over the cookie crust.

Bake until the cake is set and the center is only slightly wobbly when you gently shake the pan, about 1 hour 30 minutes. Remove the pan from the oven and let cool for 30 minutes. Transfer to the refrigerator and chill for at least 3 hours or up to 24 before serving.

LIME DOUGHNUTS

LIME DOUGHNUT
HOLES

THE DOUGH HERE IS A SPIN-OFF OF THE NO-KNEAD BRIOCHE
dough from our first book. Francisco Migoya, one of our favorite
pastry chefs, told us about "millionaire's brioche," a recipe that
uses twice the amount of butter as normal brioche. We were
immediately inspired to increase the amount of butter in our
no-knead brioche recipe, and the resulting doughnuts are light
and tender with a texture that almost melts on your tongue. One
of the great things about using no-knead dough here is that you
can reroll it without any appreciable toughening. You do need
to chill the dough between rolls, but that is a small price to pay
for being able to use all of it. The lime glaze was inspired by a
pre-dessert that we used to love at the now closed New York
City restaurant Cello, headed up by chef Laurent Tourondel. It
was a crackling mille-feuille with lime curd and a fresh lime
consommé. The flavors were haunting, and we believe that these
doughnuts are an apt tribute to that favorite dessert.

MAKES ABOUT 3 DOZEN

LIME DOUGHNUTS

MAKE THE DOUGH: In a large bowl, whisk together the flour, yeast, salt,
and sugar.

In a medium bowl, whisk together the eggs, water, and milk.
Whisk in the butter. Pour the wet ingredients into the dry ingredients
and stir with a rubber spatula until the liquid is absorbed and there are no
dry clumps. The mixture will resemble muffin batter. It may look a little
lumpy and slightly greasy, but be assured that all of the butter will be
absorbed by the time the dough rises. Cover the bowl with plastic wrap
and let it rest at room temperature for 4 to 6 hours.

Uncover the bowl and use a rubber spatula to gently loosen the
dough from the bowl. Dampen your hands with cool water and slide one
hand under one side of the dough. Fold that side of the dough into the
center and press it down gently so it adheres to itself. Give the bowl a
quarter turn and repeat the folding process two more times. After the
fourth fold, flip the dough over so the seams are on the bottom. Cover
the bowl with plastic wrap and let it rest at room temperature for 8 to
12 hours, or overnight.

DOUGHNUT DOUGH

6½ cups / 975 grams
all-purpose flour

½ teaspoon / 1.5 grams
instant yeast

3½ teaspoons / 20 grams
fine sea salt

½ cup / 100 grams **sugar**

8 large **eggs**

1 cup / 225 grams room-
temperature **water**

½ cup / 130 grams **whole
milk**

2 pounds / 900 grams
unsalted butter, melted and
cooled

JUST MIXED, BEFORE THE FIRST RISE

Uncover the bowl and repeat the folding procedure in the previous step. Put the dough onto a plastic wrap–lined baking sheet. Cover the dough with plastic wrap and pat the dough into a flattened dome. Refrigerate the dough until it is firm, at least 2 hours and up to 2 days.

Line 3 baking sheets with parchment paper and lightly dust them with flour. Remove the dough from the refrigerator and dust a countertop lightly but evenly with flour. Turn the dough out onto the floured countertop and dust it with flour. Use a rolling pin to roll the dough out to a ³⁄₈-inch (1 cm) thickness. Use additional flour if it begins to stick. Use a 3-inch (8 cm) doughnut cutter to cut out the doughnuts and put them onto the parchment-lined pans. Separate the holes from the doughnuts so they may be fried separately. Cover the pans loosely with plastic wrap and let the doughnuts proof for 1 hour. Gently ball up the trimmings from the doughnuts, put them in a bowl, cover with plastic wrap, and refrigerate until they firm up, at least 1 hour or up to 24. These trimmings may be rerolled to make additional doughnuts.

Pour 2 inches (5 cm) of oil into a large pot and heat it over medium-high heat until it reaches 350°F (177°C). Set a wire rack over a baking sheet. Put 4 to 5 doughnuts at a time in the oil and cook for 1 minute. Use a slotted spoon or a spider to flip the doughnuts over and cook them for 1 minute on the other side. Flip one more time and cook for 1 minute more. The doughnuts should be golden brown. Use the slotted spoon to transfer the doughnuts from the oil to the rack to cool. Repeat to cook the remaining doughnuts. To cook the holes, put 12 into the oil at a time and cook for 45 seconds. Use the slotted spoon to turn the holes over and cook for 45 more seconds. Some of the holes may not flip, so use the slotted spoon to stir them in the oil so they cook evenly. Transfer the holes to the wire rack.

MAKE THE LIME GLAZE: Put the confectioners' sugar in a bowl and pour in the buttermilk, lime juice, and salt. Use a whisk to stir the mixture together until it forms a smooth glaze. Reserve at room temperature and whisk until smooth before using.

Dip one side of each doughnut into the glaze, then flip glaze side up and return to the cooling rack. Grate the zest of 3 of the limes over the glazed doughnuts. Once all the doughnuts are glazed, put the doughnut holes into the bowl with the glaze and grate the zest from the remaining lime into the bowl. Use a spoon to mix the holes in the glaze and evenly coat them. Transfer the holes to the wire rack and let the glaze harden. Serve once the glaze is firm to the touch, if you can wait that long.

LIME GLAZE

Scant 2¼ cups / 250 grams **confectioners' sugar**

¼ cup / 60 grams **cultured buttermilk,** homemade (page 54) or store-bought

4 teaspoons / 20 grams **fresh lime juice**

¼ teaspoon / 1.5 grams **fine sea salt**

Rice bran oil or peanut oil, for frying

4 limes

PROOFED AND READY TO FRY

PIES &
TARTS

WHAT MAKES THIS PIE EXCEPTIONALLY DELICIOUS IS THE
combination of cooked and raw strawberries. The recipe is a riff
on the strawberry pie that Alex's grandma Kitty used to make
every Easter when he was growing up. A blend of cornstarch and
tapioca starch gel the cooked strawberry juices so that they are
just thick enough to hold everything together without getting
gummy or chewy; fresh strawberries lend their aroma and flavor
when you bite into the pie. And fresh lemon juice helps balance
all that sweet strawberry goodness. It's pretty special.

MAKES ONE 9-INCH / 23 CM PIE

KITTY'S STRAWBERRY PIE

Preheat the oven to 400°F (205°C). Line a baking sheet with parchment
paper.

Roll the pie dough into a round 12 inches (30 cm) in diameter
and line a 9-inch (23 cm) pie pan. Trim the edge so that there is a 1-inch
(2.5 cm) overhang. Roll the overhang inward and tuck underneath the
top edge so that it forms a log all the way around the pie pan. Crimp the
edges by squeezing the dough gently between your thumb and forefinger,
moving them all the way around the pan, and pierce the bottom a few
times with a fork. Put the pie shell in the freezer while the oven preheats.

Once the oven is hot, take the pie shell from the freezer and put
it on the baking sheet. Put a piece of parchment paper inside the crust,
fill it with pie weights, and bake for 20 minutes. Remove the pie weights,
reduce the oven temperature to 350°F (175°F), and bake until the crust is
a light golden brown on the bottom, about 30 minutes. Let the pie crust
cool completely at room temperature before using.

Divide the strawberries into 2 piles, one half with the prettiest
berries. Halve the prettier berries lengthwise and arrange them, cut
side down, in the prebaked pie shell. Put the sugar and salt in a medium
saucepan set over medium heat. Meanwhile, quarter the second batch of
less beautiful strawberries. When the sugar becomes an amber caramel,
carefully add the quartered strawberries. Cook, stirring, until the sugar

½ recipe **Pie Dough**
(page 212)

2 quarts / 1,200 grams
strawberries, preferably
organic

¾ cup / 150 grams **sugar**

¼ teaspoon / 1.5 grams **fine
sea salt**

2 tablespoons / 12 grams
tapioca starch

1 tablespoon / 7 grams
cornstarch

2 tablespoons / 28 grams
cold water

1 tablespoon / 15 grams
fresh lemon juice (from
½ lemon)

Whipped cream, for serving

melts and the mixture comes to a simmer. In a small bowl, mix the tapioca, cornstarch, and cold water together and then pour the slurry into the strawberries. Stir the berries as they come back up to temperature and cook until the mixture thickens and becomes glossy, about 5 minutes. Stir in the lemon juice. Remove the pan from the heat and let cool to room temperature.

Spoon the cooked berries over the top of the layer of fresh berries in the pie. Use a small spoon or rubber spatula to gently lift up some of the fresh berries and use a pastry brush to make sure that all the berries are glazed. Put the strawberry pie in the refrigerator to cool and set up for at least 3 hours before serving. Serve with freshly whipped cream.

THIS IS OUR ODE TO CLASSIC POP-TARTS. RICH TART DOUGH
mimics the cakelike texture of the original pastry, the perfect
vessel for homemade jam and thin slices of fruit. These are
equally at home for dessert as they are for breakfast.

MAKES 8 TARTS

HAND TARTS

In a food processor, combine the flour, sugar, baking powder, and salt and
pulse to blend. Add the butter and process for 5 to 10 seconds until it
forms a coarse meal. Add the cream and pulse until the mixture forms a
crumbly dough that holds together when you squeeze a bit in your hand.
Turn it out onto a floured countertop. Sprinkle the dough lightly with
flour. Starting at one end, use the heel of your hand to smear the dough
into the counter in small amounts. Do this quickly, being sure not to work
any section of dough more than once. This technique, known as fraisage,
forms flaky layers of fat and flour. Press the dough into a rough rectangle
that's about 1 inch (2.5 cm) thick. Wrap with plastic wrap and refrigerate
for at least 1 hour and up to 2 days.

Preheat the oven to 350°F (175°C). Line two 18 × 13-inch (46 × 33
cm) baking sheets with parchment paper.

Put the jam in a bowl and stir briefly to loosen. Put the sliced
fruit on a plate. In a small bowl, combine the egg yolk, milk, and a pinch
of salt and mix with a pastry brush until it is smooth. Divide the dough
into 8 equal pieces. Take one piece and roll it out into an 8 × 4-inch
(20 × 10 cm) rectangle that's about ¼ inch (6 mm) thick. Trim the edges
with a bench scraper or knife so that they are straight and even. Put
2 tablespoons of jam on one half of the rectangle and spread it in an even
layer, leaving a 1-inch (2.5 cm) border of clean pastry dough around the
entire outer edge. Layer a few pieces of fruit over the jam and fold the
opposite side over the fruit like a book. Use a fork to press the edges
together and seal the tart closed. Transfer to one of the prepared baking
sheets and refrigerate while you make the remaining tarts.

Brush the top of each tart with a thin layer of egg wash. Bake for
20 minutes and then rotate the pans, turning them from front to back and
switching racks from top to bottom. Bake until the tarts are a deep golden
brown, about 10 minutes more. Transfer the tarts to a wire rack and cool
for at least 10 minutes before serving.

3½ cups / 525 grams
all-purpose flour

3 tablespoons / 38 grams
sugar

1 teaspoon / 6 grams **baking
powder**

1 teaspoon / 6 grams **fine
sea salt**

12 ounces / 345 grams
unsalted butter

1½ cups / 360 grams **heavy
cream**

1 cup / 340 grams
Strawberry Jam (page 193)

2 large **apples,** peeled and
thinly sliced

2 large **mangoes,** thinly
sliced

1 large **egg yolk**

2 tablespoons / 32 grams
whole milk

WE AMPED UP AN APPLE PIE RECIPE BY ADDING CARAMEL SAUCE to the filling and an oatmeal streusel topping to make a pie with layers; tender cooked apples coated in rich caramel sauce, a crumbly topping, and a crisp pie shell all come together to make so much more than the sum of their parts. This triple-crusted pie has become one of our most requested recipes. A little freshly whipped cream or ice cream takes it over the top.

MAKES ONE 9-INCH / 23 CM PIE

CARAMEL APPLE PIE

MAKE THE CAKE CRUMB STREUSEL: In a food processor, combine the cake crumbs, oats, and salt and pulse 3 or 4 times to blend. Add the bitters (if using) and pulse 1 or 2 times to blend. Add the butter and sugar and pulse 3 or 4 times until the mixture forms rough crumbs. Streusel can be stored in an airtight container in the refrigerator for up to 2 weeks.

MAKE THE CRUST AND FILLING: Preheat the oven to 400°F (205°C).

Roll one disc of the pie dough into a round 12 inches (30 cm) in diameter and line a 9-inch (23 cm) pie pan. Trim the edge so that there is a 1-inch (2.5 cm) overhang. Put the pan in the freezer to chill. Roll out the second disc of dough to the same size and reserve it in the refrigerator while you prepare the apples.

Peel, core, and cut the apples into ¼-inch-thick (6 mm) slices. Put the slices in a medium bowl with the tapioca starch, cornstarch, and salt and mix well to blend. Add the caramel sauce and mix into the apples to coat evenly.

CAKE CRUMB STREUSEL

1¼ cups / 100 grams **cake or cookie crumbs**

¾ cup / 75 grams **rolled oats**

¼ teaspoon / 1.5 grams **fine sea salt**

⅛ teaspoon / 0.5 gram **Boker's Bitters** (optional)

8 tablespoons / 113 grams **unsalted butter,** diced

¼ cup / 50 grams **raw sugar**

CRUST AND FILLING

Pie Dough (recipe follows)

5 large **Honeycrisp apples**

4 tablespoons / 24 grams **tapioca starch**

2 tablespoons / 14 grams **cornstarch**

½ teaspoon / 3 grams **fine sea salt**

1 cup / 250 grams **Ginger Caramel Sauce** (recipe follows)

1 tablespoon / 16 grams **whole milk**

Remove the pie pan from the freezer and pile the apples into a mound in the pan. Cover with the second dough round and trim the edge, leaving a 1-inch (2.5 cm) overhang. Tuck the top crust over the edge of the bottom crust and crimp them together all the way around the circumference. Put the pie on a baking sheet lined with a silicone mat or parchment paper. Brush the top crust with the milk. Pile the streusel onto the top crust, gently pressing it in so that it adheres to the pie.

Bake for 30 minutes. Rotate the pie, reduce the oven temperature to 350°F (175°C), and bake until the pie is a deep golden brown, 1 hour more. Remove the pan from the oven and let cool to room temperature before serving.

PIE DOUGH

MAKES ENOUGH FOR TWO 9-INCH / 23 CM PIE CRUSTS

Great pie starts with the crust. For a combination of flavor and texture, butter is unbeatable. The food processor ensures that you don't overwork the dough in the initial mixing process, and then the process of fraisage, flattening out pieces of the dough, leaves you with flaky layers. Soggy pie crust is usually a result of undercooking, while properly cooked crust should be crisp and textured with a wonderful, slightly sweet butter flavor that rivals that of puff pastry.

2¼ cups / 337.5 grams **all-purpose flour**	¾ teaspoon / 4.5 grams **fine sea salt**
2 tablespoons / 25 grams **sugar**	8 ounces / 225 grams cold **unsalted butter,** diced
	¼ cup / 56 grams **ice water,** plus more as needed

In a food processor, combine the flour, sugar, and salt and pulse 4 or 5 times to blend. Add the butter and pulse 2 or 3 times to blend. Pour the ice water into the food processor and run the processor for 5 to 10 seconds to bring the mixture together. If it seems a little dry, add more water 1 tablespoon at a time. The dough will resemble small pebbles and hold together when you squeeze a bit in your hand.

Turn it out onto a floured countertop and sprinkle the top lightly with flour. Starting at one end, use the heel of your hand to smear the dough into the counter in small amounts. Do this quickly, being sure not to work any section of dough more than once. This technique, known as fraisage, forms flaky layers of fat and flour. Use a bench scraper or spatula to peel pieces of dough from the countertop. Gently press them into 2 compact balls of dough of about equal size, and flatten into discs no more than 2 inches (5 cm) thick. You can roll them out and use immediately or freeze for up to 1 month; alternatively, wrap the discs in plastic wrap to keep in the refrigerator for up to 1 week. Let the refrigerated dough rest at room temperature for at least 30 minutes before rolling.

GINGER CARAMEL SAUCE

MAKES A GENEROUS 3 CUPS / 750 GRAMS

This spicy caramel sauce will keep in a covered container in the refrigerator for up to a month. We love it on ice cream, folded into whipped cream, or drizzled over warm scones or bread pudding.

2¼ cups packed / 450 grams **light brown sugar**

½ teaspoon / 3 grams **fine sea salt**

1 cup / 240 grams **heavy cream**

2 tablespoons / 28 grams **unsalted butter**

4 ounces / 113 grams peeled **fresh ginger,** sliced

In a deep, medium saucepan, combine the brown sugar, salt, and cream and set over medium heat, stirring to dissolve the sugar and salt. Cook the mixture, without stirring, until it reaches 240°F (116°C) on a candy thermometer. Remove the pan from the heat and stir in the butter and ginger; this will cause the caramel to bubble up. Once the caramel has stopped bubbling, stir it until smooth. Let the sauce cool for 30 minutes. Strain out the ginger, then cover and refrigerate. The sauce may be kept in a covered container in the refrigerator for up to a month. Gently rewarm the sauce before serving.

WE CAME UP WITH THIS WHOLE WHEAT CRUST FIRST AND KNEW
it would be just right for a custard tart; the deep nutty flavors of
the shell immediately made us think of gingerbread. To augment
the flavors in this recipe, we use fresh ginger to help thicken
cream to make crème fraîche that is the basis for a creamy,
spicy filling for the pie. Tapioca starch helps keep the eggs from
curdling and holds water in suspension to ensure a silky filling.

The contrast of the wheaty crust and the soft custard makes
for a very special combination. In the wintertime it is lovely
with a tart cranberry compote, and in the summertime we
like to serve it with a large spoonful of fresh berries and their
natural juices.

MAKES ONE 10-INCH /
25 CM TART

GINGER TART

MAKE THE GINGER CRÈME FRAÎCHE: At least 2 days before you plan to
make the tart, stir together the cream, buttermilk, and ginger. Store in
a covered container at room temperature for 48 hours, until the crème
fraîche has thickened. Strain out the ginger. The ginger crème fraîche may
be stored in a covered container in the refrigerator for up to 1 week.

MAKE THE CRUST: Preheat the oven to 350°F (175°C). Coat a
10-inch (25 cm) tart pan with cooking spray and wipe it out with a paper
towel, leaving a thin film on the pan.

In a food processor, combine the flour, dark brown sugar, and salt
and pulse to blend. Add the butter and pulse 3 or 4 times to blend. In a
small bowl, use a fork to whisk together the egg, vanilla, and bitters, if
using. Add to the food processor and pulse until the mixture forms coarse
crumbs. Turn the dough out onto a lightly floured counter and press it
together into a disc about 1 inch (2.5 cm) thick. Lightly dust the top with
flour and roll out the dough into a 12-inch (30 cm) round. Transfer the
dough to the pan and gently press it into the bottom and up the sides.
Run the rolling pin over the top of the pan to trim off any excess.

(recipe continues)

GINGER CRÈME FRAÎCHE

2⅔ cups / 630 grams **heavy cream**

9 tablespoons / 130 grams **cultured buttermilk,** homemade (page 54) or store-bought

4 ounces / 113 grams **fresh ginger,** thinly sliced

CRUST

Nonstick cooking spray

1⅓ cups / 200 grams **whole wheat flour**

½ cup packed / 105 grams **dark brown sugar**

½ teaspoon / 3 grams **fine sea salt**

8 tablespoons / 113 grams cold **unsalted butter,** diced

1 large **egg,** cold

½ teaspoon / 2 grams **vanilla extract**

½ teaspoon / 2 grams **Aphrodite Bitters** (optional)

Line the tart shell with parchment paper and fill with pie weights or dried beans. Bake the tart shell for 15 minutes and remove the pie weights. Bake until the crust is set and dry, 5 more minutes. Remove the pan from the oven and let cool for 10 minutes at room temperature.

Reduce the oven temperature to 250°F (120°C).

MAKE THE FILLING: In a medium bowl, whisk together the light brown sugar, granulated sugar, tapioca starch, and salt. Add the ginger crème fraîche and whisk. Add the eggs, vanilla, and bitters, if using, and whisk just until smooth. Pour the filling into the cooled tart shell and bake for 50 minutes, until the custard is just set and still slightly wobbly in the center.

Remove the pan from the oven and let cool at room temperature for 30 minutes. Put the tart in the refrigerator and chill for at least 3 hours before serving. The tart will keep, covered in the refrigerator, for up to 5 days.

FILLING

¼ cup packed / 53 grams **light brown sugar**

¼ cup / 50 grams **granulated sugar**

1 tablespoon / 6 grams **tapioca starch**

½ teaspoon / 3 grams **fine sea salt**

4 large **eggs**

¼ teaspoon / 1 gram **vanilla extract**

¼ teaspoon / 1 gram **Aphrodite Bitters** (optional)

ONE DAY WE WERE DEBATING THE RELATIVE MERITS OF COOKIE crusts when we happened to notice a bag of pretzels on the counter. Like a bolt of lightning this pretzel crust was born, the perfect crunchy-salty match for a silky-sweet caramel tart—which made us think of candy bars, of course. The resulting tart has swirls of milk and dark chocolate ganache to make a show-stopping dessert.

MAKES ONE 10-INCH / 25 CM TART

PRETZEL CARAMEL TART

MAKE THE CRUST: Preheat the oven to 325°F (165°C). Coat a 10-inch (25 cm) tart pan with a removable bottom with cooking spray and put it on a baking sheet lined with parchment paper.

Whisk together the pretzel crumbs and flour until well blended and set aside. In a stand mixer fitted with the paddle attachment, beat the butter, brown sugar, and salt until the mixture is light and fluffy. Stop the mixer and add all of the pretzel-flour mixture. Mix on low until well combined. The mixture will resemble damp sand. Use the bottom of a measuring cup to press an even layer along the sides and on the bottom of the pan. Bake until golden brown and fragrant, 10 to 15 minutes. Let cool to room temperature while you make the caramel.

MAKE THE CARAMEL: In a medium saucepan, combine the sugar and water and set over medium-high heat, stirring gently just to dissolve the sugar. Bring to a boil without stirring and let the sugar continue to boil until it turns an amber color, swirling the pot occasionally if needed, 5 to 8 minutes. Remove the pan from the heat and tilt the pot away from you as you slowly pour in the cream and add the salt. Gradually stir in the butter. Pour the caramel into the tart pan and refrigerate for at least 1 hour to set.

(recipe continues)

CRUST

Nonstick cooking spray

2 cups / 140 grams finely ground **pretzel crumbs**

1 cup minus 2 tablespoons / 130 grams **all-purpose flour**

11½ tablespoons / 160 grams **unsalted butter,** at room temperature

⅓ cup packed / 75 grams **light brown sugar**

⅓ teaspoon / 2 grams **fine sea salt**

CARAMEL

2¼ cups / 450 grams **sugar**

1 cup / 225 grams **water**

1⅓ cups / 325 grams **heavy cream**

½ teaspoon / 3 grams **fine sea salt**

8 ounces / 225 grams **unsalted butter,** diced

MAKE THE DARK CHOCOLATE GANACHE: Put the cream in a small saucepan, set over medium heat, and bring to 167°F (75°C) on a candy thermometer, just below a simmer. Add the dark chocolate and salt and turn off the heat. Whisk until the chocolate is fully melted and the ganache is thick and smooth. Set aside, stirring occasionally while you make the milk chocolate ganache.

MAKE THE MILK CHOCOLATE GANACHE: Put the cream in a small saucepan, set over medium heat, and bring to 167°F (75°C) on a candy thermometer, just below a simmer. Add the milk chocolate and salt and turn off the heat. Whisk until the chocolate is fully melted and the ganache is thick and smooth.

Pour the dark chocolate ganache over the caramel, tilting the pan to spread it entirely across the top in an even layer. Let cool for 10 minutes at room temperature. Drizzle the milk chocolate ganache over the dark chocolate layer, warming it up slightly in the microwave, if necessary. Chill the tart in the refrigerator until it is cold and set, at least 3 hours. Slice and serve chilled.

DARK CHOCOLATE GANACHE

1 cup minus 2 tablespoons / 200 grams **heavy cream**

7 ounces / 200 grams **dark chocolate (63 to 68% cacao)**

¼ teaspoon / 1.5 grams **fine sea salt**

MILK CHOCOLATE GANACHE

⅓ cup / 75 grams **heavy cream**

2.6 ounces / 75 grams **milk chocolate**

⅛ teaspoon / 0.75 gram **fine sea salt**

PUMPKIN PIES CAN BE KIND OF BLAND AND ONE-NOTE: SWEET and squashy. In this recipe, the pastry crust and crunchy streusel topping make an appealing textural contrast to the creamy pumpkin filling. The addition of raw sugar, which doesn't melt when baked, gives it a wonderful sandy texture that is fun to eat with the creamy pumpkin filling. And while traditional pumpkin pies are flavored with sweet spices, the North African spice blend ras el hanout has so much more to offer in their place; this haunting blend of sweet and savory spices is the perfect match for the mellow flavor of pumpkin.

MAKES ONE 9-INCH /
25 CM TART

SPICED PUMPKIN PIE

Preheat the oven to 450°F (235°C). Line a baking sheet with a silicone mat.

Roll the pie dough into a round 12 inches (30 cm) in diameter and line a 9-inch (23 cm) pie pan. Trim the edge so that there is a 1-inch (2.5 cm) overhang. Roll the overhang inward and tuck underneath the top edge so that it forms a log all the way around the pie pan. Crimp the edges by squeezing the dough gently between your thumb and forefinger, moving them all the way around the pan, and pierce the bottom a few times with a fork. Put the pie shell in the freezer while the oven preheats.

MAKE THE FILLING: In a medium bowl, whisk together the pumpkin and cream until well blended but not frothy. In a small bowl, whisk together the brown sugar, salt, ras el hanout, cinnamon, and tapioca starch. Add the whole eggs and egg yolk and whisk to combine. Pour the egg mixture into the pumpkin mixture and stir with a rubber spatula until combined.

Once the oven is hot, take the pie shell from the freezer and put it on the lined baking sheet. Pour the filling into the pie shell and bake for 20 minutes. Reduce the oven temperature to 350°F (175°C) without opening the oven door. Bake for 10 more minutes.

½ recipe **Pie Dough**
(page 212)

FILLING

1 (15-ounce / 425-gram) can **organic pumpkin puree**

1½ cups / 360 grams **heavy cream**

¾ cup packed / 160 grams **light brown sugar**

1 teaspoon / 6 grams **fine sea salt**

½ teaspoon / 1 gram **ras el hanout**

½ teaspoon / 1 gram **ground cinnamon**

2 tablespoons / 12 grams **tapioca starch**

2 large **eggs**

1 large **egg yolk**

STREUSEL TOPPING

½ cup / 75 grams **all-purpose flour**

2 tablespoons packed / 26 grams **light brown sugar**

2 tablespoons / 25 grams **raw sugar**

¼ teaspoon / 0.5 gram **ground cinnamon**

¼ teaspoon / 1.5 grams **fine sea salt**

4 tablespoons / 56 grams **unsalted butter**, diced, at room temperature

MEANWHILE, MAKE THE STREUSEL: In a medium bowl, combine the flour, sugars, cinnamon, and salt and stir well to blend. Add the butter to the mixture. Use your fingers or a fork to blend everything together until it forms a chunky, sandy mixture. Use immediately or store in an airtight container in the refrigerator for up to 2 weeks.

Open the oven door and gently sprinkle the streusel over the top of the pie. Return the pie to the oven and bake for 20 more minutes. The pie should be set and jiggly in the center when fully cooked, much like gelatin. If you prefer a darker streusel, you can lightly broil the top of the pie with the oven door open to brown it for about 5 minutes. Remove the pan from the oven and let cool on the counter or on a wire rack for at least 30 minutes before serving.

10

COOKIES, CANDY & ICE CREAMS

WHEN WE WERE KIDS WE LOVED THOSE LITTLE CELLOPHANE-wrapped caramels from Kraft. They are the perfect bite and the inspiration for this recipe. We use crème fraîche instead of heavy cream to add a little bit of tang to the finished candies. They are a great blend of chewy and creamy and, yes, we have been known to chop them up and put them into pies like the Caramel Apple Pie (page 210) and substitute fresh, slightly firm peaches for a special summer treat. These caramels are also the perfect texture for folding into cookies and Rice Krispies Treats, or you could just set them out in a bowl and watch them disappear.

**MAKES ABOUT 50
(1-INCH / 2.5 CM) PIECES**

CRÈME FRAÎCHE CARAMELS

2 cups / 450 grams **crème fraîche,** homemade (page 55) or store-bought

1 cup / 315 grams **cane syrup**

1½ cups packed / 320 grams **light brown sugar**

1½ cups / 300 grams **granulated sugar**

8 ounces / 225 grams **unsalted butter,** diced

¾ teaspoon / 4.5 grams **fine sea salt**

Fleur de sel

In a large saucepan, combine the crème fraîche, cane syrup, light brown sugar, granulated sugar, butter, and salt and set over medium heat. Stir until everything is dissolved and then let the mixture cook, without stirring, until it reaches 257°F (125°C) on a candy thermometer.

Meanwhile, butter a 9 × 13-inch (23 × 33 cm) glass baking dish and line the bottom with parchment paper, letting it drape over and line two sides. (You will use the paper to lift the caramel out of the pan.) Butter the parchment paper. Once the caramel reaches 257°F (125°C), pour it into the prepared dish. Let the caramel cool to room temperature for 4 hours and then transfer to the refrigerator for at least 2 hours to firm up.

Use the parchment paper to lift the caramel out of the pan and transfer it to a cutting board. Use a sharp knife to cut the caramel into bite-size pieces and wrap each one in wax paper. Serve with fleur de sel on the side so people can season their own caramels.

COOKING BY DEGREES

Those who take their cooking seriously have a thermometer in their kitchen. These handy kitchen tools take the guesswork out of cooking many foods, especially meats. Thermometers are a must for candy making. Candies are made by cooking sugar to specific temperatures, and, as you may have noticed, caramel is one of our favorite things to make. As the sugar cooks, water evaporates and increases the concentration of sugar in the mixture. The higher the sugar concentration, the harder the finished candy. You can gauge the sugar concentration by the temperature of the sugar mixture, which is why you must have a thermometer to make candy. Frankly, the old candy thermometers drove us crazy. It was almost impossible to get one deep enough into the pan, sugar crystals had an annoying tendency to collect behind it against the side of the pot, and it was hard to read. Now, thanks to modern technology, we can all use probe thermometers. Originally designed with a long cord so that they could be inserted into meats roasting in the oven—with the mechanism safely outside—they are great for cooking sugar. You can check the temperature periodically or clip the slender probe to the side of the pan. We love them, and our caramels—whether they be creamy, chewy, or crunchy—have never been better.

Another place where temperature is incredibly important is egg cookery. People have very strong feelings about the doneness of their eggs, and there are many different dessert recipes where the possibility of an overcooked scramble is a very bad thing. The coagulation temperature of eggs is 185°F (85°C), so most internal cooking temperatures for custards fall well below that. Crème anglaise is perfectly cooked at 179°F (82°C). Baked custards are done between 170° and 175°F (77° and 79°C) to allow for carry over cooking. Soufflés need a double-check, because they have two different textures: soft and tender on the inside and firmer as you move towards the crust. They need to register 150°F (65°C) at the center and 160°F (71°C) about an inch (2.5 cm) from the surface. The internal temperature for cooking any soft meringue is also 160°F (71°C).

You'll notice that we have a penchant for toppings. Our Sourdough Coffee Cake (page 34) has a combination of gooey topping and streusel over the top. This makes for an extremely wonderful cake but can create a challenge when it comes to checking doneness. The old trick of touching the top to check for firmness will not work here. Instead, we reach for our thermometer again. Sliding the probe into the center of the cake is as easy as using an old-fashioned cake tester and much more accurate. The cake is done when the internal temperature registers 208°–210°F (97°–98°C). This is the maximum range of temperature for all cake types, whether a layer, loaf, pound, chiffon, or sponge. If your temperature has risen much above this limit, you have an overbaked cake that's likely dry with a thick outside crust and will shrink somewhat as it cools. We like to pull layer cakes at 190°–195°F (87°–90°C) to ensure a moist, tender crumb. Cheesecakes are done when their internal temperature reaches 150°F (65.5°C). Breads have a slightly different range. For soft breads with a tender crumb like brioche or rye, we look for an internal temperature of 190°–200°F (88°–93°C) and for drier, crustier loaves like baguettes or ciabatta we need a temperature of 200°– 210°F (93°–98°C).

Here's a quick guide to candy temperatures.

CANDY COOKING TEMPERATURES

TEMPERATURE	STAGE	DESCRIPTION
230°–235°F / 106°–112°C	THREAD STAGE	a glaze, a syrup, or caramel sauce
235°–240°F /112°–116°C	SOFT BALL	fudge, fondants, creams, and other softly textured candies
245°–250°F /118°–120°C	FIRM BALL	soft, chewy caramels and divinity
255°–265°F /121°–130°C	HARD BALL	marshmallows, taffy, and other pliable but firm candies
270°–290°F / 132°–143°C	SOFT CRACK	toffee, butterscotch, and other candies that gently shatter under your teeth
300°–310°F / 149°–154°C	HARD CRACK	brittles, lollipops, and other hard candies

PEPPERIDGE FARM BORDEAUX COOKIES ARE ADDICTIVE. THEY
have this incredibly crisp, light texture and a haunting caramel
flavor that stays with you for days. One day, we decided to try
and figure out how to re-create them. These cookies, while not
exactly the same, are in our humble opinion even better. They
have that addictive crisp caramelized flavor that sneaks up on
you as you eat them. Somehow they seem to get better with
every bite. They're like the French, or maybe American, version
of biscotti, perfect with your morning coffee.

**MAKES ABOUT 3 DOZEN
COOKIES**

BORDEAUX-STYLE COOKIES

8 tablespoons / 113 grams **unsalted butter,** at room temperature

1 teaspoon / 6 grams **fine sea salt**

1 teaspoon / 5 grams **baking soda**

1½ cups / 300 grams **sugar**

2 large **eggs,** at room temperature

¼ teaspoon / 1 gram **vanilla extract**

½ cup / 113 grams **rice bran oil** or canola oil

3 cups / 450 grams **all-purpose flour**

¼ cup / 65 grams **whole milk**

Raw sugar, for dusting

In a stand mixer fitted with the paddle attachment, mix the butter, salt, and baking soda on low speed. With the mixer running, add the sugar a little bit at a time. Once all the sugar has been added, turn the mixer up to medium and beat for 30 seconds until light and fluffy. Add the eggs, one at a time, and mix on medium-low until they are fully incorporated into the butter. Add the vanilla and oil and mix on medium-low until it becomes a homogeneous mixture. Add the flour and mix until just blended. Turn the dough out onto a counter and divide it in half. Roll each half into a log or shape it into a long rectangle, wrap in plastic wrap, and chill in the refrigerator until firm, at least 6 hours.

Preheat the oven to 300°F (150°C). Line 2 baking sheets with parchment paper.

Slice each log into pieces ¼ inch (6 mm) thick and lay them on the baking sheets, leaving about ½ inch (1 cm) space between each cookie. Brush the tops of the cookies with the milk and sprinkle raw sugar over them. Bake for 10 minutes and rotate the pans from front to back and switch the racks from top to bottom. Bake until the cookies are a deep golden brown, 5 to 8 more minutes. Transfer the cookies to a wire rack and let cool completely. The cookies will keep in an airtight container for up to 2 weeks.

THESE COOKIES ARE A TRIBUTE TO LINDEN'S BUTTER CRUNCH cookies. The buttery caramel bits melt as the cookies bake, creating little pockets of chewy, candied goodness. An oatmeal dough adds some heft and flavor and balances the sweetness of the candy. Unlike the original, these are soft chewy cookies that are impossible to keep in the cookie jar.

MAKES ABOUT 3 DOZEN COOKIES

TOFFEE OATMEAL COOKIES

MAKE THE TOFFEE: Line a baking sheet with foil and butter the foil.

In a small heavy-bottomed saucepan, combine the sugar and salt, set over medium-low heat, and cook undisturbed until the sugar is caramelized and a dark mahogany in color, 5 to 8 minutes.

Remove the pan from the heat. Let the hot sugar rest for 30 seconds and then slowly add the butter, swirling it into the hot sugar until it is absorbed. Pour the toffee out onto the prepared baking sheet and let cool. Once the toffee is cold, break it into small chips and reserve in a zip-top bag. The toffee will keep for up to 2 weeks.

MAKE THE COOKIE DOUGH: In a mixing bowl, with an electric hand mixer, beat the butter, brown sugar, baking soda, and salt until light and fluffy. Add the eggs one at a time, mixing well after each addition. Add the flour and oats and mix slowly to just combine. Fold in the toffee chips. Cover the bowl and refrigerate for at least 3 hours until firm.

Preheat the oven to 375°F (190°C). Line 2 baking sheets with parchment paper.

Use a ¾-ounce (21-gram) scoop to portion the cookies or measure out 1½-tablespoon balls and lay them on the baking sheets, leaving about 2½ inches (5 cm) of space between each cookie. Bake for 8 minutes, then rotate the baking sheets from front to back and switch racks from top to bottom, and cook until the centers are set and the cookies are golden brown around the edges, 4 to 5 minutes more. Transfer the cookies to a wire rack and let cool completely. The cookies will keep in an airtight container for up to 5 days.

TOFFEE

½ cup / 100 grams **sugar**

½ teaspoon / 3 grams **fine sea salt**

4 tablespoons / 56 grams **unsalted butter**

COOKIE DOUGH

8 ounces / 226 grams **unsalted butter**

1½ cups packed / 320 grams **light brown sugar**

1 teaspoon / 5 grams **baking soda**

1 teaspoon / 6 grams **fine sea salt**

2 large **eggs,** at room temperature

2¾ cups / 412.5 grams **all-purpose flour**

2¼ cups / 225 grams **rolled oats**

THIS RECIPE USES INSTANT COFFEE TO ADD A MAJOR FLAVOR punch. Modern freeze-dried coffee is nothing like the instant coffees of old; we like Starbucks VIA instant coffee because it adds wonderful flavor to baked goods. We've discovered that grinding the almonds and coffee together maximizes their effect; the fat from the nuts absorbs the coffee and helps spread the flavor through the dough.

We roll the dough out into one large sheet, bake it, and then cut out cookies while it is still warm. They pop out easily and crisp as they cool, and the odd-shaped cookies can be made into crumbs or eaten in the kitchen before company arrives. Following the recipe, we have a variation called Shaved Shortbread, an original technique that makes for an elegant presentation for a special meal.

MAKES ABOUT 3 DOZEN COOKIES

COFFEE SHORTBREAD

1 cup / 112 grams **slivered almonds**

1 tablespoon / 8.25 grams **Starbucks VIA instant coffee**

1 cup / 150 grams **all-purpose flour**

⅓ cup packed / 75 grams **light brown sugar**

11½ tablespoons / 160 grams **unsalted butter,** at room temperature

¾ teaspoon / 4.5 grams **fine sea salt**

3.5 ounces / 100 grams **white chocolate,** chopped

In a food processor, combine the almonds and coffee and grind to a powder. Transfer the powder to a bowl, whisk in the flour, and set aside.

In a stand mixer fitted with the paddle attachment, cream the sugar, butter, and salt on medium-low speed until the mixture is light and fluffy, about 4 minutes. Add the white chocolate and mix on low until just combined, about 20 seconds. Stop the mixer, add all of the flour mixture, and mix on low until just combined, 2 to 3 minutes. Wrap the dough in plastic wrap and chill in the refrigerator for at least 1 hour.

Preheat the oven to 325°F (165°C).

Remove the dough from the refrigerator, unwrap it, and put it on a lightly floured piece of parchment paper. Use a rolling pin to roll the dough out into a rough rectangle that's about 11 × 16 inches (28 × 42 cm) and ¼ inch (6 mm) thick. Transfer the cookie dough on the parchment paper to a baking sheet and bake until the cookie is golden brown and cooked through, 20 to 25 minutes. Remove the pan from the oven and immediately cut out shapes using cookie cutters, transferring the cutout cookies to a wire rack to cool completely.

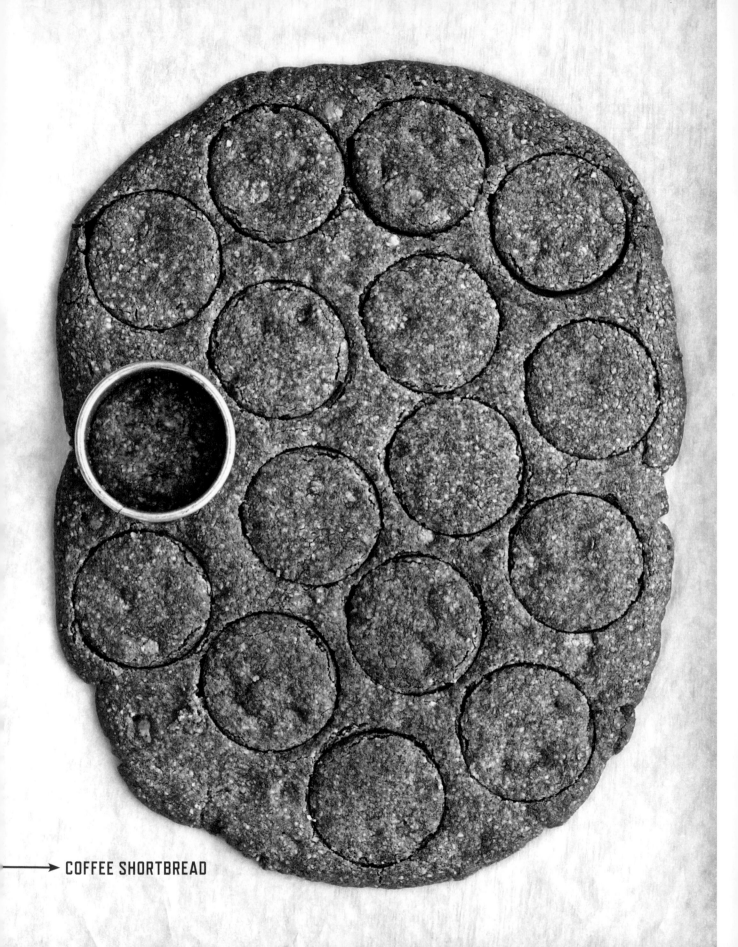

COFFEE SHORTBREAD

SHAVED SHORTBREAD

THIS IS WONDERFUL SCATTERED OVER A BOWL OF ICE
cream or pudding. We've used the curls to garnish chocolate cakes and cupcakes, or folded them into freshly churned ice cream just before putting it in the freezer to harden, giving the finished confection a great cookie flavor without any hard bits. This is also nice with warm fruit like sautéed bananas or roasted cherries, providing a nice textural contrast and a great burst of flavor.

8 tablespoons / 113 grams unsalted butter	**Coffee Shortbread trimmings,** ground into crumbs

Melt the butter in a small saucepan over medium-low heat. Once the butter is melted, continue to cook, stirring gently, until the butter solids turn golden brown and release a nutty aroma. Immediately remove the pan from the heat.

Put the shortbread crumbs into a blender. Drizzle the brown butter over the crumbs and puree until smooth. Put the puree into a pint-size plastic container and freeze for at least 4 hours.

Remove the container from the freezer, run a butter knife or an offset spatula around the inside edge of the container, and pop out the shortbread. Use a mandoline to shave the frozen shortbread and create fine shards. Alternatively, freeze the shortbread puree in ice cube trays and shave the frozen cubes using a Microplane zester. Frozen shortbread will keep in the freezer for up to 3 weeks.

KEFFELS, AN OLD FAMILY FAVORITE, ARE TENDER TURNOVER cookies that can be made with apricot or walnut filling. The original recipe called for Crisco. When we wanted to give it a makeover to ditch the trans fats and add some flavor, we decided to substitute virgin coconut oil, an ingredient that we think belongs in everyone's pantry. The oil is milled from coconut meat in a cold process that helps preserve the nutrients and polyphenols that give the oil its fragrance and flavor. It is solid at room temperature and is gaining popularity as an alternative to Crisco or lard in pastries to add flakiness and flavor. It's also wonderful in savory dishes, like Coconut Steamed Halibut (page 148), where a little bit goes a long way.

Once we added the coconut we went ahead and changed the filling, too. Tangy lemon marmalade adds a great acidic edge to balance the richness of the coconut, although if you want to make these more quickly you can easily substitute strawberry jelly for the marmalade. These keffels are a far cry from the original cookie and yet we love them just as much, if not more, because they taste delicious and we feel good about all of the ingredients that go into them.

MAKES 3 TO 4 DOZEN COOKIES

COCONUT KEFFELS
WITH MEYER LEMON MARMALADE

4 cups / 600 grams **all-purpose flour**

1 teaspoon / 6 grams **fine sea salt**

1 tablespoon / 8 grams **instant yeast**

8 ounces / 225 grams **unsalted butter,** diced

1 cup / 225 grams **virgin coconut oil**

4 large **egg yolks**

½ cup / 114 grams **Toasted Coconut Crème Fraîche** (page 240)

Granulated sugar, for rolling out the dough

½ cup / 170 grams **Meyer Lemon Marmalade** (recipe follows)

1 cup / 112 grams **confectioners' sugar**

½ cup / 57 grams **coconut milk powder** (optional; see Sources, page 248)

In a stand mixer fitted with the paddle attachment, combine the flour, salt, and yeast and mix on low speed for about 1 minute to blend. Add the butter and coconut oil and mix on low speed until the mixture resembles coarse meal. Add the egg yolks and crème fraîche and mix on medium-low until the mixture forms a smooth dough, 3 to 5 minutes. Transfer the dough to a covered container and refrigerate for at least 1 hour and up to 24 hours.

(recipe continues)

234

Preheat the oven to 350°F (175°C). Line a baking sheet with parchment paper.

Take the dough out of the refrigerator and divide it into quarters. Work with one quarter at a time, leaving the rest in the refrigerator. Generously sugar a work surface and roll out the dough (adding more sugar as needed to keep the dough from sticking) to a thickness of ⅛ inch (3 mm). Cut out 2-inch (5 cm) squares. Put ½ teaspoon of marmalade in the center of each square and fold the top third down over the marmalade and then the bottom half up, so that the cookie resembles a small log with a top seam. Gently press the ends to seal them so the filling won't ooze out the sides. Transfer the cookies to the prepared baking sheet.

Bake for 8 minutes, then rotate the pan, and bake until the cookies are just set and barely beginning to brown, 2 to 4 more minutes. Let cool on the baking sheet for 5 minutes before transferring to a wire rack to cool.

Meanwhile, in a medium bowl, whisk together the confectioners' sugar and coconut powder (if using). Transfer the mixture to a small strainer and dust the warm cookies on the wire rack. Dust them one more time when they are completely cool.

MEYER LEMON MARMALADE

Meyer lemons are sweeter and more flavorful than traditional supermarket lemons. Their season is relatively short and so we like to try to make the most of it by preserving some for when they are gone. This marmalade is one of our favorite methods of keeping the lemons in our pantry year-round. We spread it on toast and in between cake layers, put it in Hand Tarts (page 208), and swirl it through vanilla ice cream.

1 pound 1.5 ounces / 500 grams **Meyer lemons** (about 14)	½ teaspoon / 3 grams **fine sea salt**
2½ cups / 500 grams **sugar**	⅛ teaspoon / 0.25 grams **cayenne pepper**
	½ **vanilla bean**

Cut off the ends of the lemons and then cut each lemon in half and each half into 3 pieces. Cut the pieces of lemon into 4 pieces. As you cut, remove and discard any seeds. Put the lemon pieces in a stainless steel bowl that will fit inside your pressure cooker. Add the sugar, salt, and cayenne. Split the vanilla bean, scrape the seeds into the bowl, and then add the pod, too. Stir the mixture to evenly coat the lemons with sugar. Refrigerate overnight.

Put 2 inches (5 cm) of water in the bottom of a pressure cooker. Put the bowl of lemon mixture on a rack set inside your pressure cooker. Cook the lemon mixture for 30 minutes at high pressure. Let the pressure dissipate naturally. Transfer the hot lemon mixture to a heavy-bottomed saucepan set over medium-high heat. Bring the marmalade to a boil and skim off any foam that rises to the top. Cook the marmalade until it reaches 225°F (107°C).

Remove the pan from the heat and use a ladle to put the marmalade into clean Mason jars, leaving ¼ inch (6 mm) of headspace at the tops. Seal the hot jars and let them cool at room temperature. Refrigerate the finished marmalade. It will keep in the refrigerator for up to 4 weeks.

THINKING OUTSIDE THE BOX

We encourage creativity in the kitchen. The reason we aim to master culinary standards and study kitchen science is because that basic knowledge gives us the ability to be more creative. So when we have an idea that we want to explore, we also have a good idea of how to make it happen. For example, while discussing how to amp up the coconut flavor in a dish, we were struck with the idea of making coconut crème fraîche. We already knew how to make crème fraîche, so we got to work culturing some coconut milk with buttermilk—and we were happy with the results. Nonetheless, we couldn't help wondering what it would be like if we simply used a buttermilk culture, purchased from a cheesemaking supply company, to ferment the coconut milk.

We tried it and a couple of days later we had actual coconut crème fraîche. Not ones to stop when the going is good, we took the coconut crème fraîche and let it ferment for a few days at room temperature until it separated and we ended up with fresh coconut cream cheese and coconut whey. We immediately spread some of the coconut cream cheese on one of our Hand Tarts (page 208) and we were smitten.

The ideas kept coming, so we pushed this coconut experiment further. We happened to have some toasted coconut cream on hand from our recipe testing, so we decided to ferment that and see if we could make toasted coconut butter. The flavor was off the hook and there were a million uses that immediately jumped into our heads.

By running with our first thought and trying out ideas without the fear of failure, we stumbled upon some amazing ingredients that have made a big difference in our cooking. This is what happens when you bring science and creativity together in the kitchen—exploration, delicious food, and lots of fun.

CULTURED COCONUT BUTTERMILK

MAKES ABOUT 3½ CUPS / 840 GRAMS

2 (28-ounce / 794-gram) cans **coconut milk**

1 packet **buttermilk culture** (see Sources, page 248); or ¼ cup / 60 grams cultured buttermilk, homemade (page 54) or store-bought; or ¼ cup / 56 grams toasted coconut buttermilk (from Toasted Coconut Crème Fraîche and Butter, page 240)

Put the coconut milk and buttermilk culture into a bowl and whisk together. Transfer to a widemouthed Mason jar and cover with cheesecloth. Leave the mixture at room temperature for 24 hours to allow the culture to develop. The buttermilk will keep in the refrigerator for up to 2 weeks.

COCONUT CREAM CHEESE

MAKES ABOUT 12 OUNCES / 340 GRAMS

1 batch (about 3½ cups / 840 grams) **Cultured Coconut Buttermilk** (recipe opposite)

Put the buttermilk in a covered container and let it sit at room temperature for 48 hours.

Line a colander set over a bowl with 4 layers of damp cheesecloth and pour in the buttermilk. Cover with plastic wrap and refrigerate for 2 hours. Twist together the top of the cheesecloth gently so that more whey will be pushed out and then let it continue to drain for at least 8 more hours. When the cream cheese is thick, transfer it to a covered container and refrigerate. The coconut cream cheese will keep in the refrigerator for up to 2 weeks.

TOASTED COCONUT CRÈME FRAÎCHE AND BUTTER

MAKES ABOUT 2 CUPS / 480 GRAMS CRÈME FRAÎCHE
AND ⅔ CUP / 150 GRAMS BUTTER

1 cup / 50 grams large **unsweetened coconut flakes**

1¾ cups / 420 grams **heavy cream**

4 tablespoons plus 1 teaspoon / 60 grams **cultured buttermilk,** homemade (page 54) or store-bought

Scant ¾ teaspoon / 2.15 grams **fleur de sel** (1%)

Preheat the oven to 350°F (175°C). Line a baking sheet with parchment paper. Spread the coconut flakes out on the baking sheet and toast the flakes for 8 minutes. Remove the pan from the oven and let the flakes cool to room temperature.

In a stainless steel bowl, combine the toasted coconut, cream, and buttermilk and stir to combine. Cover the bowl with plastic wrap and let the mixture sit at room temperature for 24 hours to culture.

After 24 hours, the cream will have thickened and developed a slightly sour aroma. Put the bowl in the refrigerator for 6 hours. At this point the toasted coconut crème fraîche can be strained and stored in a covered container in the refrigerator for up to 1 week.

To make butter, remove the coconut crème fraîche from the refrigerator. Let it sit out at room temperature for about 1 hour or until it comes to 50°F (10°C). Transfer it to a food processor and churn the crème fraîche for 1 to 2 minutes until it is whipped and separates into butter and buttermilk. Turn the food processor off and scrape down the sides. Pulse the butter and buttermilk several times and then scrape the contents into a clean bowl. Refrigerate the butter globules in the buttermilk overnight.

The next day, drain the butter in a fine-mesh sieve, reserving the buttermilk for another use. Put the butter into a clean bowl. Use your hands to knead the butter together, squeezing out any buttermilk. When the butter mass comes together and is mostly free of buttermilk, sprinkle it with the salt and quickly knead it into the butter. Pack the butter into a clean porcelain ramekin and cover with a piece of parchment paper and then plastic wrap. Refrigerate the butter and reserve the buttermilk for culturing coconut buttermilk.

NUT BRITTLES ARE A GREAT CHOICE FOR ICE CREAM MIX-INS
because their light texture makes them easy to chew even when
frozen. Brittle is made by adding baking soda to caramel just
before pouring it out of the pan. The baking soda reacts with
the sugar acids and makes the caramel foam. The caramel sets
around the foam and all those tiny air bubbles are what make
the finished candy brittle. We use guar gum instead of eggs or
starch to thicken the ice cream base. It gives it a great, almost
chewy texture. This makes a chunky ice cream that needs no
extra toppings or sauces; it's a perfect dessert eaten all by itself.

MAKES ABOUT 1 QUART /
1 LITER

WALNUT BRITTLE ICE CREAM

MAKE THE WALNUT BRITTLE: Butter a baking sheet and line it with a
silicone mat. In a medium saucepan, combine the 8 ounces butter and
the glucose and set over medium heat to melt the butter. Add the sugar
and salt, stirring the mixture just to combine. Cook, without stirring,
until the mixture reaches 280°F (138°C) on a candy thermometer. Add
the walnuts and stir just to combine. Continue to cook until the mixture
reaches 305°F (152°C). Remove the pan from the heat and add the baking
soda, stirring well to completely incorporate. Pour the brittle onto the
prepared baking sheet and let it cool completely before breaking it into
pieces. The brittle will keep in an airtight container for up to 2 weeks.

    MAKE THE ICE CREAM: Put the milk and 3 cups (500 grams) of
the walnut brittle in a blender and puree until smooth. Sprinkle in the
salt and the guar gum, and puree until the guar gum is evenly dispersed.
Strain the ice cream base through a fine-mesh sieve into a container,
cover, and refrigerate for at least 4 hours.

    Freeze in an ice cream maker according to the manufacturer's
instructions. Fold the remaining walnut brittle into the ice cream before
transferring it to a covered container to harden in the freezer for at least
4 hours before serving.

WALNUT BRITTLE

8 ounces / 225 grams **unsalted butter,** plus more for the pan

2 teaspoons / 20 grams **liquid glucose** or light corn syrup

1 cup plus 2 tablespoons / 225 grams **sugar**

¾ teaspoon / 4.5 grams **fine sea salt**

4⅔ cups / 375 grams **walnuts,** toasted (see page 39)

¾ teaspoon / 3.75 grams **baking soda**

ICE CREAM

3⅔ cups / 1000 grams **whole milk**

¾ teaspoon / 4.5 grams **fine sea salt**

1½ teaspoons / 4.5 grams **guar gum** (0.3%)

THE BANANAS FOR THIS ICE CREAM ARE COOKED FIRST IN A dark caramel to help break them down and release some of their natural pectins and then pureed into a tapioca-thickened pudding. The tapioca starch helps bind the free water in the mixture, which helps prevent the formation of large ice crystals, aka freezer burn. The resulting ice cream is incredibly smooth and creamy. Serve a scoop of this alongside Caramel Cake (page 191) or Sourdough Coffee Cake (page 34) or serve it in a sundae with Ginger Caramel Sauce (page 213), Shaved Shortbread (page 233), some Roasted Nuts (page 39), and whipped cream.

MAKE ABOUT 1 QUART / 1 LITER

BANANA CARAMEL ICE CREAM

1¼ cups / 250 grams **sugar**

5 medium **bananas,** sliced (17 ounces / 475 grams after peeling)

3 tablespoons / 18 grams **tapioca starch**

¾ teaspoon / 4.5 grams **fine sea salt**

2 cups minus 1 tablespoon / 500 grams **whole milk**

2 cups plus 1 tablespoon / 500 grams **heavy cream**

Put the sugar in a medium saucepan and set over medium heat. Cook until it starts to melt and caramelize, about 5 minutes. Gently swirl the pot to evenly caramelize the sugar and continue to cook until the sugar is fluid and a dark amber, about 5 minutes. Remove the pan from the heat and carefully add the bananas. Put the pan over low heat and cook, stirring with a silicone spatula, until the bananas are cooked through and break down, about 5 minutes. Remove the pan from the heat and let cool for 10 minutes. Transfer to a blender and puree until it is smooth. With the blender running, sprinkle in the tapioca starch and salt and blend until the mixture forms a thick paste, about 15 seconds.

In a medium saucepan, combine the milk and cream and bring to a simmer. Remove the pan from the heat, turn the blender on low, and slowly drizzle the hot mixture into the blender. Once all of the milk mixture has been added, increase the blender speed to medium and blend for 1 minute. Turn the blender off and strain the ice cream base through a fine-mesh sieve into a bowl. Put the bowl into an ice water bath and let cool completely. Refrigerate the mixture for 4 hours.

Freeze in an ice cream maker according to the manufacturer's instructions. Transfer the ice cream to a covered container and let it harden in the freezer for at least 4 hours before serving.

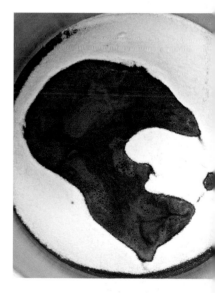

SLOWLY CARAMELIZING THE SUGAR

MIXING THE BANANAS
INTO THE CARAMEL

BANANAS COOKED
IN CARAMEL

THIS RECIPE IS NATURALLY THICKENED BY THE ACIDITY OF THE lemon curd and the crème fraîche, so there is no need to add any extra stabilizers like eggs or starch to make the ice cream smooth. As a result, it has a bright flavor that is a nice match with fresh fruit or Kitty's Strawberry Pie (page 206).

MAKES ABOUT 1 QUART / 1 LITER

LEMON-GINGER ICE CREAM

Scant 1⅔ cups / 380 grams **Ginger Crème Fraîche** (page 215)

6½ tablespoons / 80 grams **sugar**

¼ teaspoon / 1.5 grams **fine sea salt**

Microwave Lemon Curd (page 189)

In a medium bowl, combine the crème fraîche, sugar, and salt and stir to dissolve the sugar and salt (you may need to warm the crème fraîche slightly in order to do this). Add the lemon curd and stir to combine. Put the mixture in a covered container and let it rest in the refrigerator for at least 4 hours to let the flavors develop.

Freeze in an ice cream maker according to the manufacturer's instructions. Transfer the ice cream to a covered container and let it harden in the freezer for at least 4 hours before serving.

SOURCES

AFTELIER PERFUMES

(510) 841-2111
www.aftelier.com
Chef Essences: all natural, food-grade essential oils for the kitchen and bar

ALL-CLAD METALCRAFTERS LLC

(800) 255-2523
www.allclad.com
Heavy-duty cookware

ANSON MILLS

(803) 467-4122
www.ansonmills.com
Organic heirloom corn and rice products

BLIS, LLC

(616) 942-7545
www.blisgourmet.com
Caviar, barrel-aged maple syrups and vinegars

BOB'S RED MILL

(800) 349-2173 customer service
www.bobsredmill.com
Specialty grains, flours, beans, baking ingredients, with organic and gluten-free products

BRADLEY TECHNOLOGIES CANADA INC.

(800) 665-4188
www.bradleysmoker.com
Electric smokers

THE CHEF'S WAREHOUSE

(718) 842-8700
www.chefswarehouse.com
Specialty ingredients for chefs, pastry chefs, and passionate home cooks, including glucose and Valrhona chocolate in bulk

CHOCOSPHERE

(877) 992-4626
www.chocosphere.com
Fine chocolates and cocoa powders

COOKSHACK, INC.

(800) 423-0698
www.cookshack.com
Electric smokers

HOMEGOODS

www.homegoods.com
Inexpensive cookware, ingredients, tableware

IRINOX

www.irinoxusa.com
Blast chillers, shock freezers

ISI

www.isinorthamerica.com
Cream and soda siphons

JB PRINCE COMPANY, INC.

(212) 683-3553
(800) 473-0577
www.jbprince.com
Kitchen tools, equipment

JUST TOMATOES, ETC.

(800) 537-1985
www.justtomatoes.com
Dehydrated and freeze-dried fruits and vegetables

KING ARTHUR FLOUR

(800) 827-6836 customer service
(802) 649-3717 baker's hotline
www.kingarthurflour.com
Flours, baking necessities

KITCHENAID

(800) 541-6390
www.kitchenaid.com
Mixers and food processors— our favorite

KITCHEN ARTS AND LETTERS

(212) 876-5550
www.kitchenartsandletters.com
Arguably the best cookbook store in the world

KORIN JAPANESE TRADING COMPANY

(212) 587-7021
www.korin.com
Japanese knives, grills, charcoal, kitchen equipment

LE CREUSET

www.lecreuset.com
Quality cookware that looks great on the table

LE SANCTUAIRE

(415) 986-4216

www.le-sanctuaire.com

Spices, spice blends, specialty ingredients, high-end china, equipment

LODGE MANUFACTURING COMPANY

(423) 837-7181

www.lodgemfg.com

Cast-iron cookware

MICHAEL'S STORES, INC.

(800) 642-4235

www.michaels.com

Their cake-decorating section is a good source for specialty pastry items, including glucose and glycerin

MITSUWA MARKETPLACE

www.mitsuwa.com

Quality chain of Japanese supermarkets with an online store for Asian ingredients

NEW ENGLAND CHEESEMAKING SUPPLY COMPANY

(413) 397-2012

www.cheesemaking.com

Supplier of cheesemaking supplies and cheese and buttermilk cultures

O OLIVE OIL

(888) 827-7148

www.ooliveoil.com

Delicious and flavorful California olive oils, including lemon olive oil, and specialty vinegars

POLYSCIENCE

(800) 229-7569

www.polyscience.com

Our favorite immersion circulator, vacuum sealers, the smoking gun, other specialty kitchen equipment

RARE TEA CELLAR

www.rareteacellar.com/

Teas, vinegars, oils, flavorings, and kombu

RED BOAT FISH SAUCE

http://redboatfishsauce.com

Our favorite fish sauce

TERRA SPICE COMPANY

(574) 586-2600

www.terraspicecompany.com

Spices, spice blends, powdered dairy, coconut powder, dried and freeze-dried fruits and vegetables, sweeteners, flavorings

VALRHONA CHOCOLATE

www.valrhona.com

One of our favorite chocolates

WARING PRO

www.waringpro.com

Professional-quality kitchen appliances for the home, including deep fryers, blenders, waffle makers, and meat grinders

WEBER-STEPHEN PRODUCTS CO.

(800) 446-1071 customer service
(800) GRILLOUT grill line

www.weber.com

Grills

WHOLE FOODS MARKET

www.wholefoodsmarket.com

Specialty cuts of meat; if you don't have access to a great local butcher, we've found that Whole Foods will cut to order and is a good source for specialty cuts

WILLIAMS-SONOMA

(877) 812-6235

www.williams-sonoma.com

Spice blends, kitchen appliances and equipment (including immersion circulators), ingredients, small wares

WINSTON INDUSTRIES

(800) 234-5286

www.winstonind.com

CVap, a great tool for controlled-temperature cooking

ACKNOWLEDGMENTS

THERE'S NO SUCH THING
as a solo book project.

It takes an entire team of people to make this happen. As with the first book all of this would have been impossible without our agent, Sharon Bowers; our editing team at Clarkson Potter, Rica Allannic and Ashley Phillips; copy editor Kate Slate, who caught all of the mistakes that we missed and helped give us a fresh perspective on things; art director Jane Treuhaft and designer Laura Palese, for pulling everything together into a beautiful package; production editor Christine Tanigawa and production manager Derek Gullino, for taking care of the manuscript and overseeing the printing. And we have to thank the entire team at Clarkson Potter for all of their help in getting this book into your hands.

We'd like to acknowledge all of our clients and the readers of both our blog and our first book, *Ideas in Food*. You're the ones who got us here and changed the idea of writing books from a dream into reality. We'd like to thank the culinary community at large for its friendship and support. We are lucky to work in a group that believes in helping each other find answers and share ideas. With that in mind, a big thank-you to Karyn and the staff at our local Williams-Sonoma in Langhorne, Pennsylvania, for generously loaning us props and linens for the photo shoots.

Finally we'd like to thank our families for their love and continuous support. We couldn't have done it without you.

INDEX

Note: Page references in *italics* indicate photographs.

ABOUT THE AUTHORS

AKI KAMOZAWA &
H. ALEXANDER TALBOT,

authors of *Ideas in Food* and owners of a consulting business by the same name, have worked with both individual chefs and companies such as No. 9 Group in Boston, Fourth Wall Restaurants in New York City, Frito Lay, and Unilever. Their company grew out of their blog, ideasinfood.com, which they started in 2004 as a way to record their daily work in restaurant kitchens. Winners of an IACP Award in 2012 for their recipe writing, they have been featured in the *New York Times*, *Popular Science*, *Food & Wine*, and *Saveur* and speak regularly at professional conferences around the world.